The Best Beginner's Guide to Horses and Ponies for Kids

I0818485

The Best Beginner's Guide to Horses and Ponies for Kids

Everything You Need to Know about Breeds, Riding, Safety, and More!

Kirsten Lee

Sky Pony Press
New York

Sky Pony Press books may be purchased in bulk at special discounts for sales promotion, corporate gifts, fund-raising, or educational purposes. Special editions can also be created to specifications. For details, contact the Special Sales Department, Sky Pony Press, 307 Fifth Avenue, 4th Floor, New York, NY 10016 or info@skyhorsepublishing.com.

Sky Pony® is a registered trademark of Skyhorse Publishing, Inc.®, a Delaware corporation.

Visit our website at www.skyponypress.com.

10 9 8 7 6 5 4 3 2 1

Manufactured in China, January 2026
This product conforms to CPSIA 2008

Library of Congress Cataloging-in-Publication Data is available on file.

Cover design by Kai Texel
Cover images by Getty Images

Interior image credits: Shutterstock and Getty Images, unless otherwise noted. Kirsten Lee, pages xii, 36, 50, 51, 85, 98, 99, 111, 117, 131, 138, 150, 154, 174, 191, 192. Susan Antinozzi, page 142.

Print ISBN: 978-1-951934-40-8
Ebook ISBN: 978-1-951934-39-2

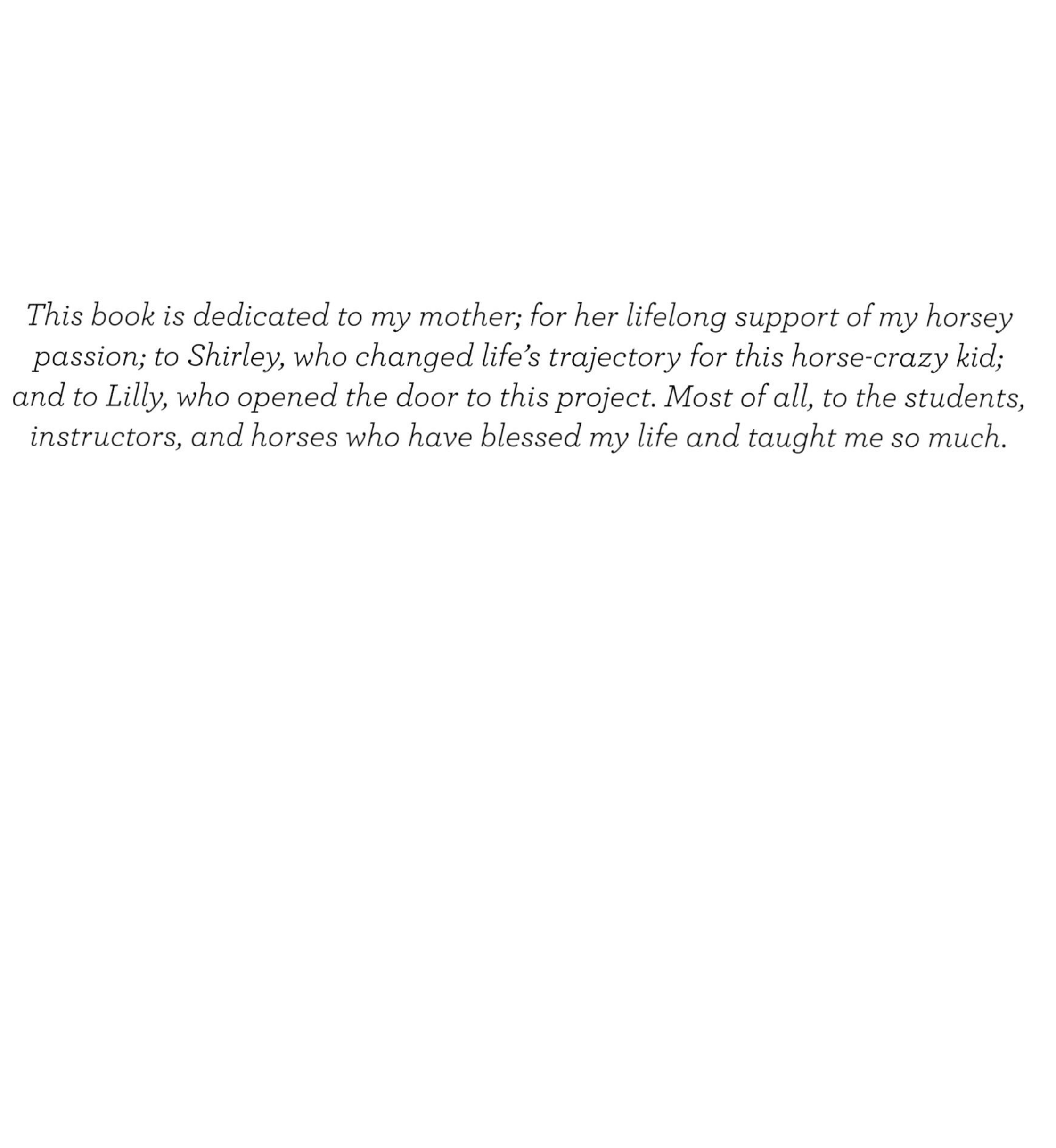

This book is dedicated to my mother; for her lifelong support of my horsey passion; to Shirley, who changed life's trajectory for this horse-crazy kid; and to Lilly, who opened the door to this project. Most of all, to the students, instructors, and horses who have blessed my life and taught me so much.

CONTENTS

Introduction

Welcome to my barn-in-a-book!

I already know you are horse crazy. How do I know? Because I am too. I've spent my whole life learning about horses: training them, showing them, having adventures with them . . . and teaching horse-crazy kids like you all about them. This book is going to teach you everything you need to know to get started right, and what to do next.

In this book, you will learn all about horses. You will discover how they helped us make history. You will explore their bodies and minds, inside and out. You will learn how to ride, train, and care for them. You will survey horse shows and horse sports all around the world. You will even learn how you can have a career with horses. Most importantly, you will understand *why* we do what we do with horses.

Throughout this book you will find projects, prompts, and questions. You will create a horse journal, and be encouraged to record, write, question, create, and draw. This will help you remember everything you are learning. It is ok if you get

answers wrong—this is how we learn. Just read the chapter again to find the answer. I'll also ask questions that have more than one right answer. These will get you thinking in new or different ways.

You can read this book straight through, or skip to the chapters that interest you most. If you do not think you are interested in horse breeds now, come back to it later. If you need to learn a fact about riding or horse care, skip to that chapter.

Read each chapter more than once. For example, read the riding chapter before and after each lesson or ride.

Draw a picture to go along with what you learn. Some kids think more clearly in pictures than in words. Even if you are not what we call a "visual learner," drawing a picture will help you remember what you learned.

Most importantly, make this book your own. If it is your own personal copy, highlight explanations to help you remember or make notes in the margin to remind you to dig deeper on things that interest you. If this is a borrowed book, or you do not want to mark up your copy, take notes in your horse journal.

There are some things you can do alongside reading to learn the most you can about the horses we love. If this were school, we'd call it extra credit. When it is horses, we all love extra!

Your Horse Journal

Start a book of notes and new ideas. Athletes call it a log book. Scientists call it a field notebook. Artists call it a sketchbook. If you're a horse rider, you're already an athlete. Now you can be an artist and a scientist as well!

Write down what you learn. Draw pictures and diagrams. If you take lessons or have a horse of your own, keep a diary of what happens in your rides. Write stories about imaginary lessons or rides, too. These will help you remember and progress faster.

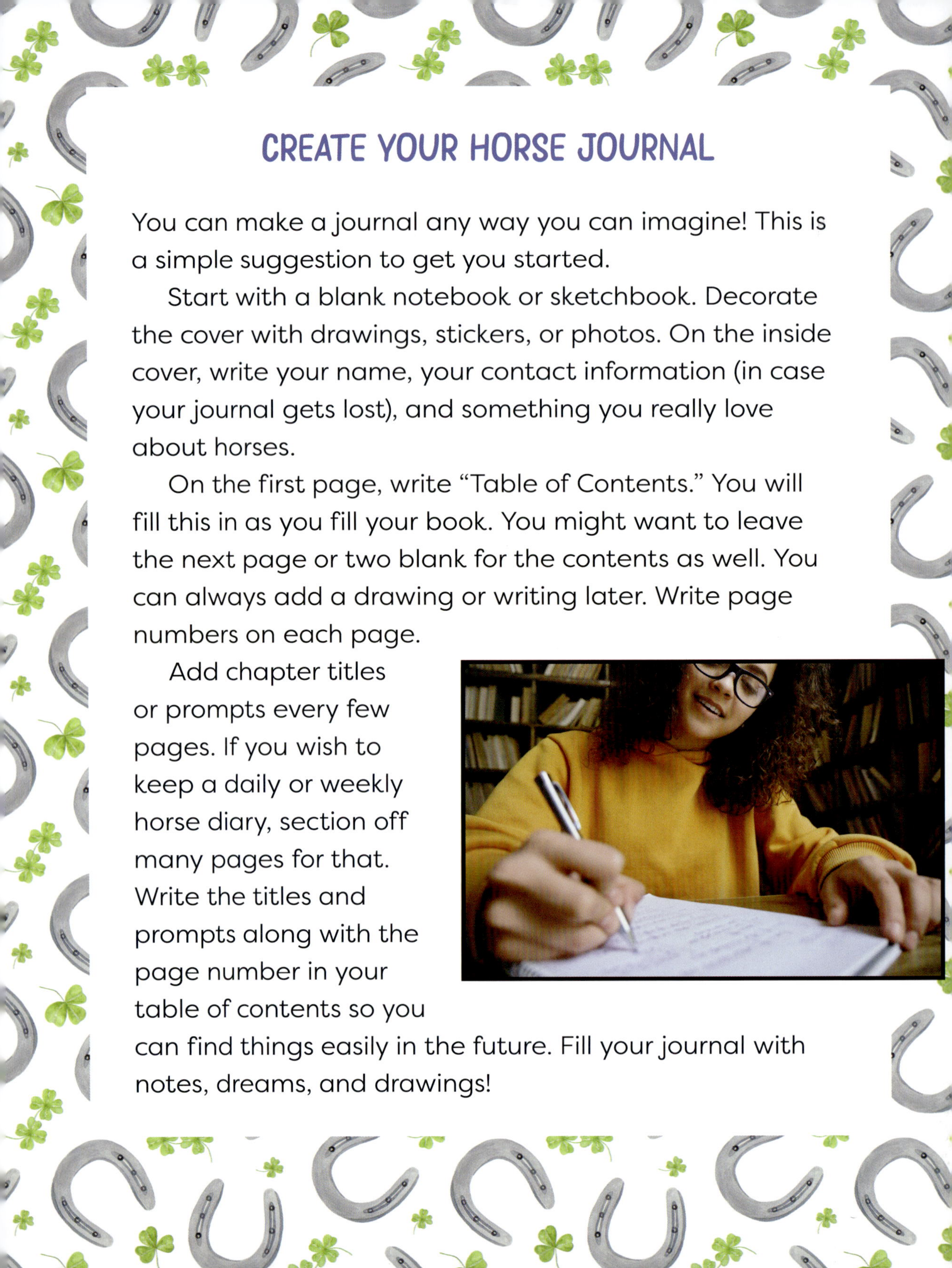

CREATE YOUR HORSE JOURNAL

You can make a journal any way you can imagine! This is a simple suggestion to get you started.

Start with a blank notebook or sketchbook. Decorate the cover with drawings, stickers, or photos. On the inside cover, write your name, your contact information (in case your journal gets lost), and something you really love about horses.

On the first page, write "Table of Contents." You will fill this in as you fill your book. You might want to leave the next page or two blank for the contents as well. You can always add a drawing or writing later. Write page numbers on each page.

Add chapter titles or prompts every few pages. If you wish to keep a daily or weekly horse diary, section off many pages for that. Write the titles and prompts along with the page number in your table of contents so you can find things easily in the future. Fill your journal with notes, dreams, and drawings!

Ideas for chapter titles and prompts:

- Notes from books
- Dreams and goals
- Wish lists for tack stores
- Books you have read
- Books you want to read
- Checklists for horse shows
- Your dream horse
- Stories you write
- Favorite breeds
- Unusual facts
- Horsey quotes

If you ride, own, or imagine you own a horse, add these prompts:

- Things your horse loves
- Things your horse dislikes or fears
- Notes from your lessons
- Goals for your next lesson
- Goals for the year
- Training plan
- Rider fitness program (out of the saddle)
- Your competition plan
- Health, dental, and veterinary records
- Shoeing records
- Monthly expenses

What prompts can you think up?

The Stable in Your Mind: Visualization

Did you know that when you imagine doing something, it is almost like you're practicing in real life? Scientists call this "visualization." Your favorite sports stars do this to improve their performance.

If you do not have a horse or take lessons, you can use your imagination to create your own riding stable in your mind. When you do get in the saddle in real life, you will already have the benefit of hours of visualization.

If you already ride, you can still practice seeing pictures and playing movies of good horsemanship in our minds. This is a way to progress on days when you cannot get to the barn. Try it: see it, imagine it, and do it. Track the ways you improve in your next lesson in your horse journal.

The more you can use each of your senses to learn, the more you will remember.

- *See* words and pictures, or watch a video or real-life lesson.
- *Hear* the instructor, or even your own voice reading this book out loud.
- *Touch* by writing notes or drawing pictures and diagrams.
- *Smell* the sweet scent of horses and saddle leather.
- *Taste* the crunch of carrots or apples . . . or imagine more tastes of your own.

Take Your Book to the Barn

Of course, books aren't meant to be left on a shelf! Take all the great information you will learn out into the stable and the riding arena. Regular lessons with a qualified teacher are the best way to learn how to ride and care for horses.

If you already take lessons, congratulations! Some of the things your instructor teaches may seem different than what you read here. If your teacher does things differently than we talk about in this book, that's OK. It is not "wrong." Ask her the reasons why she does what she does—you might be surprised to learn the answer! Always be polite and respectful.

Always ask permission before doing things differently. There are many ways to do the same thing with horses. Everyone has reasons for doing what works for them.

As you get more experience, you will learn what works best for you and the horses you ride. What makes sense when you think about it? What brings good results when you actually do it? Both are important to consider.

The one thing that is absolutely nonnegotiable is abuse of either horses or humans. Bullying, cruelty, and violence are *never* acceptable. You will learn how horses express pain, fear, confusion, and helplessness. If there is any question in your mind that abuse might be taking place, talk to a trusted adult immediately.

On Safety and Horses

There are almost as many ways to handle, ride, and house horses as there are humans to think them up! The reality remains that horses are large, fast-moving animals that can kill. Their size, speed, and flight instinct can be deadly if humans let down their guard.

Despite being so large, horses are unexpectedly fragile. They can injure themselves on seemingly safe objects around the farm, by playing too roughly, or by inconsiderate riding.

The only way to stay "perfectly" safe is to stay away from horses. But where is the fun in that? The next best way to stay safe is to learn correct techniques and good habits from the beginning, which you will learn here. We do not want to scare

you. We want to teach you the best ways to have fun with your horse while keeping you both safe.

A Few Words About Words

Horse-crazy kids can be both girls and boys! The horses we love and ride are both male and female as well. Throughout this book we will use "he" and "she" randomly, unless we are talking about a specific individual.

When we talk about a "horseman" or "horsemanship," we are referring to a horse-crazy kid of any gender or age. Anyone that works with horses is called a "horseman." A horseman can be a boy or a girl.

We will also refer to "your" horse. This refers to any horse you love, even if you do not ride or own him. If there is not a real horse in your life, imagine one. What color, breed, and height is he? What is his name? What is his personality? The more real you can make him, the more easily you will visualize and learn about riding and horsemanship.

On Your Mark, Get Set, Go!

So saddle up and get ready to learn about everything Equus! (That's the scientific word for horse. Say "EK-wiss.") When you finish this book, you won't be an absolute beginner anymore!

REAL HORSES, REAL RIDERS

As you read through these chapters, you will meet a wide variety of horses and hear what their people have to say. Some ride for a living, some ride for fun, and all are horse crazy like you! Some people have asked that they be mentioned by their first name only, or by an imaginary name, but the stories are all true.

As you read their stories, see if you can recognize similar pieces in your own life. There is not one single road to achieving your horse dreams. In fact, everyone's horse dreams look unique, just like them!

You may live in the city or on a farm. You may have a horsey family. Or perhaps you're the first in your family to fall head over heels for horses. Whatever your circumstances, you have already started "writing" your own personal horse story that will continue for the rest of your life.

1

Why We Love Horses

You already know you love horses. But have you ever thought about why? Yes, they are beautiful, athletic, and generous. Their spirit, intelligence, and power capture our hearts. People have fallen in love with these qualities for centuries.

Horses have also helped humans build civilizations throughout history. Throughout times of war and peace, horses have been the key to creating the world as we know it. Let's go back in time and follow horses around the world from their very beginning all the way to today. Along the way, we will learn facts about the horse's nature that will help us become better horsemen.

There are lots of long, scientific words in this section. Take your time and sound out the syllables. You can also ask your parents or teachers for help. They will be excited to know you are studying your favorite animal!

Horses in Prehistory

Around 55 million years ago, North America was like a jungle. Lush foliage grew in the hot, swampy environment. The first ancestors of the horse appeared. Hyracotherium (hi-RACK-o-THEER-ee-um), also known as Eohippus (EE-oh-HIPP-us) and the dawn horse, were about the size of a dog. Like dogs, these little animals scampered about on padded toes. Their short teeth munched leaves and soft vegetation. Their patterned coats helped them hide from predators in thick underbrush.

How did these shy little creatures become the majestic horses we love? Over millions of years, the environment gradually changed. Hyracotherium had to change to survive. Some adaptations, or physical changes, allowed the animals to mature and breed and create new family lines. Family lines that couldn't adapt became extinct (died out). Through this crooked path spanning millions of years, little doglike Hyracotherium evolved into *Equus caballus* (EK-wiss ka-BAHL-us), today's horse.

> Many natural history museums have detailed displays which show the evolution of the horse as eras passed and the environment changed. See if there is one near you! Many museums also have online exhibits you can freely explore.

Over the next 15–23 million years, the world's climate became hotter. The jungle dried out and gave way to forests. Mesohippus (MEE-zoh-HIP-us), meaning "middle horse" appeared, with teeth that were larger and greater in number than those of their ancestors. They could eat the twigs and tougher vegetation that grew in place of the lush jungle.

One of the toes on each leg shrank. Those that remained grew longer: better able to run fast on the harder ground of the forests. They fled from predators with the speed of a deer and were about the same size.

Over millions of years, grassy plains gradually began to replace forests. Mesohippus developed into Miohippus, and then into Merychippus (MARE-ee-CHIP-us). As the forest disappeared, they were no longer able to hide from danger in the underbrush. Their eyes grew wider apart to spot predators on the wide-open plains. Their legs grew longer. Their side toes became smaller, and they began to run on their middle toes. They grew a strong hoof—so different from Hyracotherium's padded toes! Their teeth became even

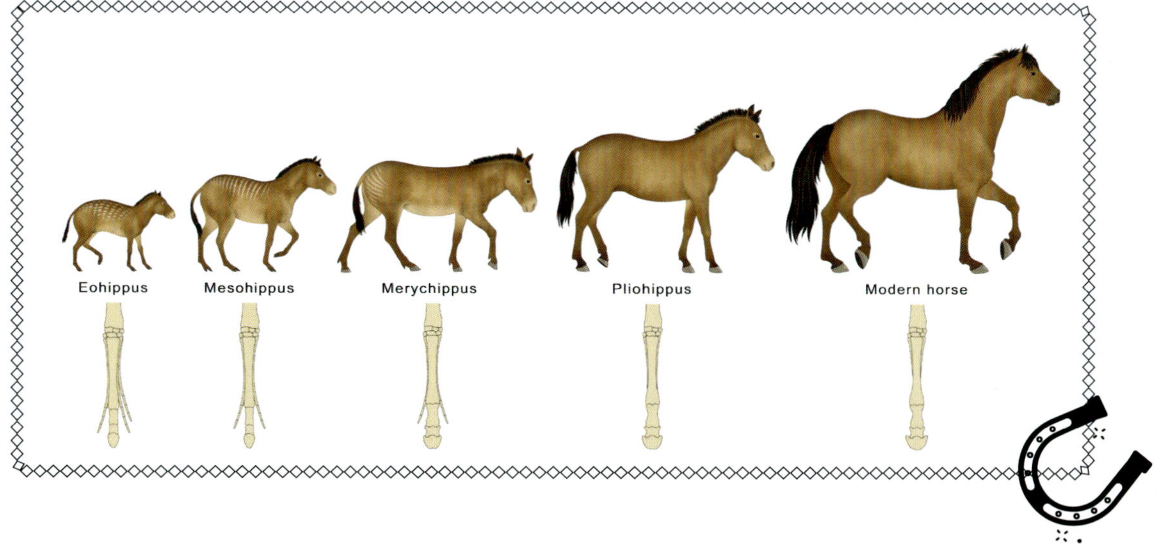

stronger. They could chew the tough grass that covered their world like a blanket.

Merychippus gradually evolved into Pliohippus (PLEE-oh-HIP-us). Pliohippus was about the size of a small pony. While some still had three toes, many fossils show only the center toe remaining, just like modern horses.

Not all of the equids in the family tree were small. The Giant Cape Zebra (*Equus capensis*) fossils found in South Africa were over 18.2 hands high!

Horses and their closest relatives are the only living creatures on earth with a single toe!

Roughly 5 million years later, Pliohippus grew into *Equus caballus*. They did not look like the horses you see today. They were short and stocky. They had light brown coats with a light muzzle and belly. Their manes were spiky and stood up straight. *Equus caballus* was the ancestor of all modern horses and their relatives such as zebras and donkeys.

How have scientists been able to piece together such a clear picture of possible horse evolution? Bones and fossils of primitive horses have been found in abundance. Using a process called carbon dating, scientists are able to tell the age of a bone or fossil. Like detectives, they can paint a picture using other clues, such as the type of stone, soil, or fossils found near it. Because horse fossils are so plentiful, scientists have been able to create a solid theory of equine evolution.

Scientists who study the ancient past are called "paleontologists." If you love horses, science, and mysteries, this might be the perfect career for you!

THE HAGERMAN HORSE

The Hagerman horse (*Equus simplicidens*) is one of the oldest species of Equus. They roamed the western United States between 4 and 3 million years ago.

The Hagerman Horse is the state fossil of Idaho. You can see the real skeleton at the Hagerman Fossil Beds National Monument! Scientists believe the Hagerman horse had a brown neck and shoulders, with a striped top line (crest and back) and haunches, like a zebra.

Horses and the First Humans

While *Equus caballus* was evolving, North America and Asia were connected by the Bering Land Bridge, a stretch of land between Alaska and Siberia. Our horses' ancestors were able to move back and forth between the continents.

The Bering Land Bridge allowed humans to cross into North America for the first time. They discovered that horses were a plentiful supply of food. Humans became horses' primary predator.

When the last ice age ended, melting glaciers covered the Bering Land Bridge for the last time in history. Horses could no longer cross between the continents. Scientists believe humans hunted horses until none were left in North America.

Even though horses were extinct in North America, they thrived throughout Europe, Asia, and Africa. Horses moved

HORSE HISTORY

Early *Equus caballus* probably looked very much like the Tarpan, or European wild horse. The last known Tarpan died in 1909. Genetic testing shows that the Tarpan is the ancestor of all living horses.

The Asiatic wild horse of Mongolia, the takhi, looks very similar to the Tarpan. "Takhi" means holy horse or spirit in Mongolian. They are also called Przewalski's horse (shi-VAL-skee's horse), after the Russian explorer who first described them to Europeans.

Scientists think the takhi was the last horse that evolved in the wild, without human interference. Even so, modern genetic research has shown that while it is a relative, the takhi is not an actual ancestor of modern horses.

The last wild takhi in Mongolia died in the 1960s. Thanks to captive breeding programs in zoos, the takhi was revitalized and released back into the wild steppes of Mongolia. The takhi are the only truly wild horses in the world today.

freely across the continents to new lands. Herds grew in size and strength.

Humans continued to hunt horses as a source of food. Cave paintings show horses as prey in hunting scenes. It is thought that humans first kept their own horse herds solely for meat and milk. As horrible a thought as it sounds to you, tens of thousands of years ago, humans did what they had to do to survive.

The first people thought to domesticate (tame and raise) horses were the Botai. This culture lived in Kazakhstan (north central Asia) around 5,500 years ago. Pottery jars uncovered at historical sites contain traces of mare's milk. Long-buried horse teeth showed wear that suggests use of a bit and bridle.

Genetic tests have proven that modern horses did not descend from the Botai horses. What does this tell us? Even though the Botai left us the oldest evidence of domestication, other cultures also developed relationships with horses that carried down through the centuries.

Some of the first art that we know about was painted on the walls of caves throughout Europe, Asia, and Africa. Those early artists used charcoal, ground rocks, and minerals to paint horses that look very similar to the takhi. Because the caves are dark and protected from the weather, these paintings can be seen today. Cave paintings help connect us to our artistic ancestors. They show how humans relied on horses even then.

Humans began to realize they could use horses' strength and endurance for more than food. Initially, horses dragged loads or carried goods on their backs. Once the wheel was invented, horses were able to move faster and pull heavier loads. Eventually, humans learned to ride.

HORSE STORIES

Imagine being a horse-crazy kid in the days of our ancestors! Picture yourself looking at the horses your family raised for food and seeing their beauty and fire. Imagine watching the gentleness between a mare and her foal, or between two equine best friends nibbling each other's withers, or racing across the plains together.

Can you imagine wanting to befriend them? Can you imagine having the courage to slide onto one of their broad backs for the very first time? Imagine you were that first rider. Write a story about that first ride in history.

How to Write a Horse Story

- Pick your theme or topic. Choose something you think would be fun, interesting, and exciting.
- Imagine your characters—human and horse. Who is the most important (main character)? Who are the supporting characters? What are their names? How do they look and act? What are their personality quirks?
- Map out the plot. What will happen at the beginning, the middle, and the end?
- A smooth story is a boring story. What are the challenges your characters will face? How will they triumph? What adventures will they have on the way? The greater the challenges, the more interesting the story will be!
- Write your story. Start with an interesting description or exciting event to capture your reader's interest right away. Continue through your characters' challenges and adventures.
- As you learn more about horses, you can add new vocabulary and facts to your descriptions. Bring everything together in a fulfilling ending.
- Edit your story. Reread your story several times. How can you make it stronger, more exciting, or more heartfelt? Fix any spelling and grammar errors. You can ask parents, friends, and teachers for their help.
- Illustrate your story. You will learn how to draw horses in the next chapter!

Horses in Agriculture and Industry

Horses have been important in agriculture for thousands of years. Their size and strength meant that they could do the work of many humans.

Horses pull plows to till fields for crops. They haul produce and crafts to markets. They transport goods to new lands.

As humans invented new machines to make farm work easier, horses provided the power. They pulled threshing machines to harvest grain. They powered mills to grind grain into flour. Even their manure is useful to fertilize land for better crops.

Horses helped build early cities, transporting all the supplies needed to build new structures and feed the workers. Once the cities were developed, horses were vital for bringing food from distant farms. Daily city life was powered by the transportation that horses provided long before the invention of cars.

We hear the term "horsepower" when talking about cars and engines. Horses were the original horsepower! James Watt, a Scottish engineer during the Industrial Revolution, defined one horsepower as the amount of energy it takes a horse to lift 550 pounds one foot above the ground in one second.

When coal was discovered as a source of energy, horses were needed once again. Small but sturdy ponies pulled carts full of coal in mines deep underground. On the surface, massive draft horses pulled heavy loads of coal wherever it needed to go.

Throughout history, horses have helped humans to develop civilizations all around the world. No wonder we have such a strong bond!

Horses in War

Early civilizations designed chariots, two-wheeled carts pulled by horses. Chariots allowed warriors to aim bows and spears with speed and accuracy. An army with well-trained charioteers and strong, fast horses could conquer new territory with ease.

Mounted warriors played an important role as well. The height and speed of horses gave their riders a huge advantage over unmounted opponents.

Saddles began as simple padding. Over time, a framework, called a tree, was added. For thousands of years, saddles had no stirrups.

Invention of the Stirrup

Riders and warriors began to experiment with ways to keep their feet and legs stable. The first stirrups were simple loops that hung from the saddle. Riders would slide their big toe or their entire foot into the loop.

The first solid stirrups appeared around 300 CE. How do we know? Images of riders using stirrups appear in Chinese art from that time. Soon other cultures were designing their own versions of stirrups.

Stirrups allowed warriors to be much more accurate with their weapons. They allowed riders to travel further without getting tired. This simple invention revolutionized horsemanship!

Medieval Horsemanship

Horses were vital to every part of life during the Middle Ages. Different

The Kikkuli Text is the name of the very first written guide to horses that we know of. It was written on clay tablets in what is now Turkey over 3,000 years ago! It describes how to train and care for chariot horses.

The Art of Horsemanship is the first horse book that discusses riding. It was written around 2,400 years ago by the Greek general, Xenophon. He stressed the importance of using patience, understanding, and kindness when working with horses. Many of his teachings are still in use today.

Imagine archaeologists (people who study the past) finding your horse journal hundreds of years from now. What do you think they would learn? Would you write your journal differently if you knew it would be in a museum one day?

types of horses even had different names, depending on the jobs they performed. Just as someone today might have both a car and a pickup truck to do different jobs, people living in the middle ages might have more than one horse.

The Myth of the Massive Warhorse: Books and movies describe destriers as tall and mighty. In actually, they were only around 15 hands high. How do we know this? Suits of equine armor hint at the shape and size of the horses who wore it.

The destrier (DES-tree-ay) was a powerful warhorse trained for heavy combat. Destriers carried full armor as well as an armored knight. A courser was a fast, athletic horse suited to hunting, light combat, and speedy transportation.

The palfrey was a gentle horse with comfortable gaits that made traveling long distances more enjoyable. A rouncey was a sturdy horse with a good temperament who could be used for farm work as well as transportation. The sumpter was strong and level headed, perfect for carrying heavy supplies for war or commerce.

Horses in the Renaissance

As the Middle Ages came to a close, people became more interested in culture, art, and intellectual learning. While horses were still used extensively in farming, war, and commerce, horsemanship began to be seen as an art form. Horses were

used in elaborate performances in front of royalty.

Horsemen began to examine their techniques and training more closely. Countries established high-level schools of horsemanship. Many of these schools, such as the Spanish Riding School in Vienna, Austria, are

Horsemen wrote down their methods in books. Throughout the centuries, these books have been translated and become more readily available. You can read the wisdom of the masters of horsemanship in their own words. Check your library. Ask your librarian how to request an interlibrary loan for books your branch does not carry.

still active today. They teach the same classical principles of horsemanship that were taught at their creation hundreds of years ago.

Return to the Americas

In 1519, horses finally returned to the American continent. The conquistadores of Spain were the first to bring horses on ships. Some of these horses escaped to freedom, and eventually became the Mustang breed that still roams the American west. Others were stolen by daring Indigenous people, who then created their own herds. Over time, horse populations grew to great numbers.

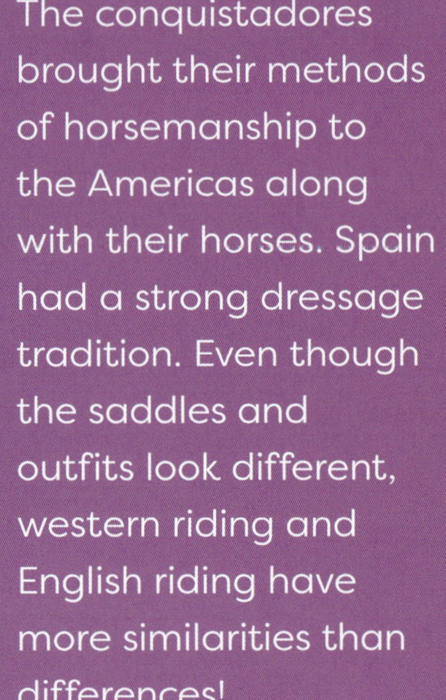

Other immigrants also brought horses from their homelands. Horses became a vital partner in building the Americas, as they already were in Europe, Asia, and Africa.

Horses Today

In many developing countries, horses still provide the horsepower for farming and transportation. Even in our world full of cars and computers, horses still have important jobs.

They help police officers keep the peace in major cities. They are used in therapy to help people overcome disabilities. They pull tiny houses on wheels called caravans. Horses are needed on the vast cattle ranches that provide the beef that feeds us.

Horses can help protect the environment. They pull farm and logging equipment in fragile ecosystems where truck tires would cause damage. They drag internet cables in rugged, remote areas that trucks cannot access.

The horses we love who helped build history are still working next to us today.

Horses have never stopped evolving. Humans have had a big hand in that. They selectively breed mares and stallions that both have the traits they are looking for, such as strength or speed. Today's horses look different than early *Equus caballus*. Many are much larger. Their longer necks and legs allow more athletic movement. They can run faster and jump higher than their ancestors would imagine.

Before humans, environment was the strongest force that shaped horses' evolution. This included predators, food sources, and climate. What environmental forces do you think might be shaping horses today?

Pop Quiz: Which Methods Have Researchers Used to Uncover Horse History?

A. Genetics
B. Google
C. Carbon dating
D. Findings on location
E. The library
F. Watching television
G. Historical artwork

In this chapter, we talked about A, C, D, E, and G. However, a good researcher is always looking for clues and new sources of good information, so all of these answers could be correct!

You can think like a scientific researcher. While you are exploring, consider the reliability and motivation of your source. Cross-reference facts; that is, see if multiple sources list the same information. Look for evidence or proof that the information is correct. Ask your parents, teachers, or librarians for help.

2

The Horses We Love

You probably already have a favorite breed of horse. Do you dream of racing the wind on a fiery Arabian? Of soaring over huge fences on a Thoroughbred or Hanoverian? Or perhaps gliding along a shady mountain trail on a Tennessee Walker?

The Oklahoma State University database documents over 200 recognized horse breeds worldwide. Wow! But have you ever thought about what makes a breed a breed?

What's in a Breed?

A breed is a group of horses that have been developed to have certain characteristics that can be passed down reliably to their offspring. Breeds usually have distinct conformation (structure), features, and temperaments suited to a particular purpose. Some breeds are associated with certain colors. Other breeds, such as Pintos, are defined by their color alone. Breeds are

DIFFERENT TYPES FOR DIFFERENT TASTES

"Type" describes variations within a breed. Types developed to suit a particular need or job. Here are some typical types that appear in different breeds.

Stock: Perfect for ranch work—stocky build, sensible temperament, and sturdy enough to carry a heavy cowboy and his gear on a long day's work. Usually "cow-y," horseman's speak for having strong instincts to work cattle.

Hunter: Ideal for a day galloping and jumping across the countryside, now more likely to test their abilities in the show ring. Athletic and elegant, with an efficient, ground-covering movement called "daisy cutting."

Park: Flashy and high-headed with extreme knee and hock action. Shown in saddle seat or fine harness classes.
Sport: Extremely athletic, with expressive gaits for the upper-level dressage arena and the "scope," or ability, to soar over big fences.

The mighty Clydesdale and the tiny Shetland pony were both developed in Scotland to help humans pull heavy loads. Clydesdales pulled massive machinery through thick soil in farmer's fields. Shetland ponies pulled carts full of coal through dark, narrow mine shafts. How do they look different? What do they have in common? Why do you think that might be?

governed by an organization called a registry, which keeps track of the horses in a "studbook."

The idea of breeds is fairly modern. People throughout history have taken pride in the horses they love. They tracked pedigrees and bloodlines of successful horses. The idea of putting similar bloodlines into registries or studbooks while excluding horses outside those bloodlines didn't come about until the 1700s. In the case of many breeds, it was far later.

Breeds are still changing today. As people's needs and tastes change, breed standards follow. Many breeds show different "types" within the same registry. Each type has slightly different conformation or temperament features that make them more successful for a particular purpose.

Artificial Selection

You now know how horses developed over time into the incredible creatures we love today. The climate and the environment shaped changes in their bodies and behavior. Horses that couldn't adapt to these changes did not survive long enough to have babies. This is called "natural selection."

Once humans domesticated horses, they were able to control mating. If they wanted a faster horse, they would breed their swiftest stallion to their speediest mares. If they needed more strength to help farm crops, they would mate their largest, most cooperative animals. This is called "artificial selection."

Wealthy owners could import exotic new stallions and mares to improve the herds back home. Some stallions traveled from farm to farm throughout a region. However, when the fastest means of transportation was the horse itself, mare owners were usually limited to nearby stallions.

Genes are the structures that control the traits that parents pass to their offspring. Scientists studying horses have discovered specific genes that control factors like appearance, temperament, and disease. This helps horse breeders make smart choices to increase the chance they will breed their perfect foal. Scientists still have much to discover. Do you love horses and science? Maybe you will become an equine geneticist and make new discoveries!

Cooler . . . Warmer . . . *Hot*-bloods!

Sometimes, horse people talk about horses like they are temperatures. "She's a hot one," they might say. Or "I rode the new warmblood yesterday." As you will learn in chapter 3, all healthy horses have an internal temperature around 101 degrees. What gives?

The horses we call hot-blooded horses are lean and speedy, often with feisty, energetic personalities. Arabians and Thoroughbreds are considered "hot-blooded." Cold-blooded horses are big and stocky with docile temperaments. Draft horses are cold-blooded. As you have probably guessed, a warmblood can be a mix of a hot-blood and a cold-blood. Warmblood also refers to a group of sport horse breeds developed in Europe and America. A warmblood has the athleticism of the hot-blood, with added sturdiness and calmness from their cold-blooded parent.

A Brief Look at Common Breeds

While there are more than 200 recognized horse breeds around the world, several breeds are especially popular for riding, showing, and working with people. In this section, you will meet some of the most common horse breeds and explore what makes each of them unique.

Arabian: The Arabian is one of the oldest breeds. Most breeds developed throughout history contain Arabian genetics. Arabians have been bred for centuries for speed, endurance, and breathtaking beauty. They have distinct "dished" profiles, with bulging foreheads and

Most horses have eighteen sets of ribs, but Arabians only have seventeen. They also have one fewer vertebra in their back and in their tail. This may contribute to their high tail carriage.

concave faces. They "flag" their tails, carrying them high, especially when they are excited.

Thoroughbred: Thoroughbreds are exceptional athletes. While they are known best for their racing speed, they also excel in other disciplines as well. Thoroughbred blood has contributed to many warmblood breeds, as well as to the Quarter Horse. All Thoroughbreds who ever lived descended from only three stallions: the Godolphin Arabian, the Darley Arabian, and the Byerley Turk.

Quarter Horse: The American Quarter Horse descended from the Spanish horses of conquistadores and the Thoroughbreds of the English colonists. They are named for their bursts of unbeatable speed over a quarter mile. Quarter Horses tend to be sturdy and tough.

Morgan: Morgans are another breed "made in America." All Morgans descended from a single stallion named Figure, who belonged to a Vermont schoolteacher named Justin Morgan. Morgans are strong and versatile, and love to please.

Appaloosa: Appaloosas were developed by the Nez Perce tribe to be swift and fearless in battle. While some can be solid-colored, they are known for their distinctive spotted coats, striped hooves, and white "sclera" around the iris in their eyes. Europe and Asia have also given rise to spotted breeds, such as Denmark's Knabstupper.

Standardbred: While most racing breeds are ridden by jockeys, Standardbreds pull carts called sulkies. They race at a fast trot or at a "pace," another two-beat gait where the legs on the same side of their body move together. Standardbreds' sturdiness and calm temperaments make them good riding horses. Many sulky racers move on to careers in endurance racing. Breeds developed in other countries for harness racing include England's Norfolk Trotter and Russia's Orlov Trotter.

Gaited Horses: All horses walk, trot, canter, and gallop. Some breeds have even more gaits! Their legs move in different patterns that result in an exceptionally smooth ride. Gaited horses are popular for trail-riding and are especially beloved by people with back or hip problems. Gaited breeds developed in the Americas include the Saddlebred, Tennessee Walker, Missouri Foxtrotter, Rocky Mountain horse, Peruvian Paso, and Paso Fino. Perhaps the oldest known gaited horse is the Icelandic, known as far back as the Vikings!

Warmbloods: We've talked about warmbloods as crosses of hot- and cold-bloods. But "warmblood" is also the name given to very specific breeds, often from different European countries. Many registries have strict acceptance rules, beyond descending from registered bloodlines. Stallions must pass a rigorous performance test to be allowed to breed. Only registered mares, and in some cases, registered Thoroughbred and Arabian mares, produce foals that are eligible for registration.

All foals are inspected and judged for conformation and potential. These strict rules have resulted in high-caliber equine athletes. Popular European warmbloods include Hanoverians, Trakehners (Trah-KAY-ners), and Belgian Warmbloods.

Draft Horses: While draft horses were originally bred to work farmland and transport heavy goods, they can also make reliable riding horses. You might recognize Clydesdales from billboards or the Super Bowl. Belgians, Percherons, and Shires are other popular drafts. The golden American Cream and the Sugarbush Harlequin Draft were developed in the United States.

Smaller draft breeds are very popular riding horses, often with stout bodies and calm temperaments. These include the Norwegian Fjord, the Vanner (also called colored cob or Gypsy), and the Haflinger.

The Friesian breed, developed in the Netherlands, is often considered to be a light draft. Friesians have been used for war, transportation, farm work, and riding. With their jet-black coats, long manes and tails, feathered legs, and animated gaits, Friesians are very popular in movies.

Ponies: Good things come in small packages! A pony is any equine under 14.2 hands. History has seen many specific pony breeds. Most of the ponies you will meet were originally developed in Ireland and the United Kingdom, including Shetlands, Connemaras, and Welsh ponies. The United States is the birthplace of the Pony of the Americas, or POA, which has distinctive Appaloosa coloring. European breeders are developing the German Riding Pony, a small version of a sporting warmblood that stands 15.1 or smaller.

Color Breeds: Some breeds show a particular coat color, but registration is based on pedigree. For example, all Norwegian Fjords are a variation of dun, but not all duns are Norwegian Fjords. Many Akhal-Tekes have coats that look shiny, even metallic. Most Appaloosas have spotted coats, but some are solid-colored.

Color breeds register horses with particular coat colors, regardless of their bloodlines. Palominos and Pintos are examples of color breeds. A horse might be “dual registered” in both a color registry and a bloodline-based registry.

HOW TO DRAW A HORSE

Choose a photograph of a horse you like. (Artists call this your reference image.) Start with big, rough shapes. Sketch lightly so you can change or erase lines later. Draw a shape that the horse's body and legs will fit into. This might be a square or a rectangle.

Draw large ovals for the shoulders and haunches. Draw a triangle the size and shape of the neck and ears. Draw another triangle for the head, with circles for the cheek and muzzle. If you are not familiar with the terms for the horse's parts we discuss here, skip ahead to chapter 3.

Pay attention to the different proportions, that is, how long or short, or near or far, shapes and lines are to each other. Draw long, upside-down triangles for the legs, with circles for the knees and hocks, and small triangles for hooves.

Now improve the details. Sketch the lines of the back inside the top of the box you first drew. Sketch the curve of the neck and belly. These details reveal the horse's breed and individual characteristics.

What do you do if the horse is at an angle, or moving? Follow the same steps. What shape fits around the horse's body and legs? Draw that. How does the neck relate to that shape? How does the triangle of the head relate to the neck?

Pay attention to the shapes of the negative spaces (the empty shapes around the horse). Negative shape drawing can help you get even more accurate.

Once you feel confident sketching from a reference photo, try sketching from life, or from your imagination. Put your sketches in your horse journal. Drawing is like riding . . . and any other skill. It requires lots and lots of practice before it starts looking good, so sharpen your pencil and start sketching!

Threatened and Endangered Breeds

As human needs and tastes change, breeds may become less popular. The Livestock Conservancy is an important organization that tracks breeds that are in danger of dying out. Some endangered breeds, such as the Shire, the Suffolk Punch, and Cleveland Bay, were introduced to the United States from other countries. Other breeds, such as the Marsh Tacky and Florida Cracker, were developed on United States pastures.

REAL HORSES, REAL RIDERS

Jim is one of the many modern farmers who believe in the value of good old-fashioned horse power! When he planned his farming operation, he invested in two rare Suffolk Punch mares. The breed was developed in England for heavy farm use. Jim's mares were not only well-trained for farm work, but they were also bred to a majestic Suffolk Punch stallion.

Jim knew he wanted to farm with horses. He decided to seek out Suffolk Punches due to their endangered status. Jim knew he could achieve his goals *and* help add to an endangered population. What a win-win situation!

Making the Grade

So far, we have talked about purebred horses: steeds who have whose parents are both the same breed. But most horses are a combination of breeds. We call these wonderful horses crossbreds, or "grade." Despite the humdrum name, grade horses can be the best! They can combine the strongest traits of their parents, even if their parents are grade horses themselves. In fact, many grade horses were probably bred from the same mindset that historical horse lovers used: breed the best mare you have to the best stallion you can afford for the job you need accomplished.

Many if not most of your favorite lesson horses can be classified as grade. This does not mean we love them any less!

There is an old horseman's saying, "You cannot ride papers." The perfect horse gets the job done, no matter who his parents are!

Free as the Wind

You have learned that Mongolian takhi horses, also called Przewalski's horses, are the only true wild horses today. But many herds of ownerless horses freely roam on all continents except Antarctica. These are "feral" horses, whose domesticated ancestors escaped or were released.

In the United States, herds of mustangs thrive in the west. Herds of feral ponies, including the famous Chincoteague ponies, live on barrier islands along the east coast.

Rescue Me!

As people began to see horses as companion animals rather than livestock, horse rescues and sanctuaries became more widespread. A sanctuary is usually a farm dedicated to allowing animals to live out their lives in peace and safety. A rescue usually takes in animals that are in danger, nurses them back to health, and then sells or adopts them to safe, loving homes. Rescue horses might be anything from grade to the finest pureblood who fell on bad luck and hard times.

Many rescued horses make fine mounts once they have been rehabilitated. Even if you do not adopt a horse, there are plenty of ways you can help! Consider volunteering for a horse rescue, providing grooming services, cleaning stalls, or doing office work. Some rescues will let you volunteer as a rider. You can also raise money to

HUMANS HELPING HORSES

Keiona was deeply moved by stories of the horses affected by Hurricane Katrina in 2005. She learned that an animal welfare charity was offering matching donations.

Keiona did her research and learned the organization was legitimate and did wonderful work around the globe. Keiona created a painting (of a horse, of course!) and posted it on social media. Within hours, Keiona sold the painting and donated the money. The charity matched her donation, doubling the funding going to hurricane horse rescue!

donate. If you have a barn of your own, you can even consider fostering a rescue. There are almost as many ways to help as there are horses who need helping!

A Weighty Topic

What breed can carry the heaviest rider? Contrary to popular belief, draft horses are not necessarily good weight carriers. Although they are the largest equines, they were bred to pull heavy loads, not to carry heavy riders. Look for a smaller horse with a sturdy build and plenty of "bone" (horseman's lingo for thick, strong legs). Stock type Morgans and Quarter Horses are good examples. Less common breeds that are also good weight carriers include Icelandics, Haflingers, and Norwegian Fjords.

3

Horses Inside and Out

Do you love to look at horses? Perfect! That's what this chapter is all about. We all love to look at beautiful, powerful horses. This chapter will teach you how to look in a way that helps you describe and understand the horse in front of you.

You will learn the names of different horse parts, colors, and markings. You will learn how to know when your horse is healthy and when she is sick. Let's get to know horses from the outside in!

Horses on the Outside

Horses are mammals, just like us. We share most of the same bones, muscles, and organs, just organized differently in our bodies. Some of a horse's body parts have the same names as people parts, such as foreheads, nostrils, mouths, and ears. Some parts, like gaskin, stifle, or ergot, are completely different!

Diagram the parts of a horse in your journal. Memorize a few parts a day, then find those parts on a picture of a horse or on a real horse.

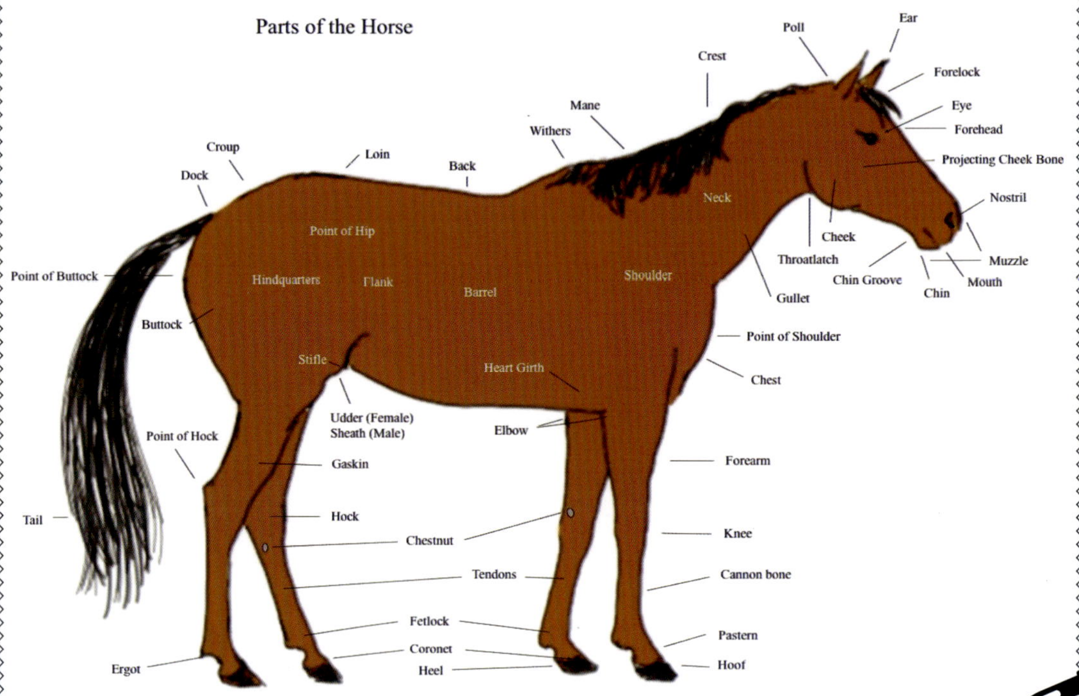

Parts of the Horse

The Big Picture

A general description that we overhear in barn aisles or read in sales listings might sound like this: "*Shasta+++/,15.3 Arabian mare, made show champion, bay with a star." This description is packed with information about the horse. You have already learned about common breeds. Let's unpack the rest piece by piece.

Height

Horses are measured from the ground to the top of their withers in units called "hands." A hand is four inches. If you hold your hand sideways, you can see where that unit came from! Horses are measured with an L-shaped measuring stick for accuracy.

We break fractions of hands down into inches and add that after a decimal point. Our "15.3" mare in the example stands 15 × 4 inches + 3 inches, that is, a total of 63 inches, at the withers. "Ponies" are under 14.2 hands when they are fully grown. "Horses" stand 14.2 hands and over. Miniature horses must be 8.2 hands (34 inches) or under.

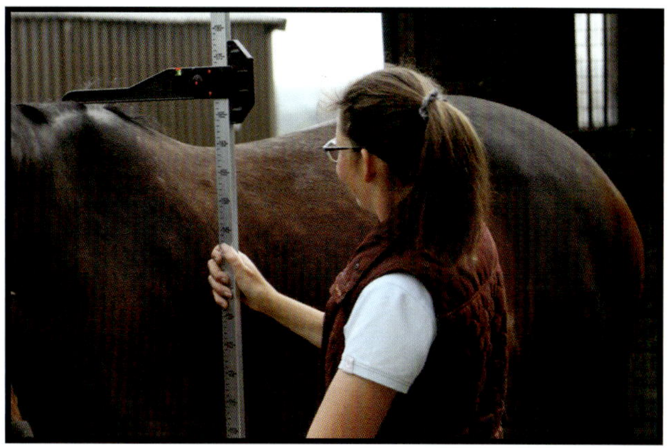

BIG AND SMALL

- Fans of carriage driving have yet another height classification: VSE, which stands for Very Small Equine. A VSE must be less than 9.3 hands (39 inches).
- The tallest horse ever recorded was Big Jake, a Belgian gelding. He was 20 hands, 2.75 inches. The smallest horse ever recorded, Thumbelina, was only 17 inches tall!

The height of a horse is not a good indicator of how much weight he can carry, nor his athletic ability. Large horses tend to be more prone to physical problems.

WHO'S WHO IN THE HERD

Stallion: an adult male horse able to reproduce
Mare: an adult female horse
Gelding: an adult male who has been neutered or castrated (cannot reproduce)
Foal: a baby horse under one year old
Weanling: a foal who no longer nurses his mother
Filly: a female under four years of age
Colt: a male under four years of age
Dam: a mother horse
Sire: a father horse

Neutering mares who have complications with their breeding cycles is possible, but uncommon. As with dogs and cats, the surgery is called "spaying." So far, the horse world hasn't come up with its own name for a spayed mare.

Training and Accomplishments

Horsemen are proud of their animals. It comes as no surprise that we have a special vocabulary to talk about it! Our sample mare from the listing above, Shasta, is "made," which means she is considered very well trained. Other words that also mean well-trained are "seasoned," or "school master." The opposite would be "green," meaning untrained or inexperienced, regardless of age.

Some breed registries have their own designations of accomplishment. The asterix in front of her name in the listing tells us Shasta was born outside the United States and imported. The symbols after her name tell us she has earned the Supreme Honor and Supreme Merit awards, both measures of success in the Arabian show ring.

A Good Horse is Never a Bad Color

Horses come in a rainbow of colors. Some horses are several colors at once! Color depends on the genetics from its sire and dam. While the sun can cause lightening of hair and a shaggy winter coat may look slightly different, the basic color of the horse's coat remains the same throughout its life. The one exception is gray, and even that is determined by genetics.

When we talk about a horse's color, we are looking not only at the color of the horse's body, but also what we call the "points." The points include the horse's legs, mane, tail, muzzle, and the rims of the ears.

A Rainbow of Browns

The most common horse color we see is brown. If a brown horse has black points, we call him a bay. A light brown horse is called a sandy bay. A red brown horse is called a blood bay. A dark brown horse is called a dark or mahogany bay.

> "A good horse is never a bad color" is an old saying. It means color doesn't have an effect on personality or performance. You can have a favorite color, but remember, "beauty is only skin deep!"

If a brown horse has brown points, we call her a chestnut. A dark brown coat with a dark mane and tail is called a liver chestnut. A sorrel has a brown coat with a light brown or blonde mane and tail.

Sometimes it is difficult to tell if a horse's points are black or dark brown, particularly if the horse's body appears to be black. We call this horse "dark bay or brown." Only if we are certain all portions of the coat (other than markings) are black do we call him "black."

Beyond Brown

A roan horse has white hairs mixed in with the base coat. A red roan is a bay intermixed with white. A strawberry roan is a chestnut mixed with white. A blue roan is black mixed with white.

A pinto looks like someone painted large blotches over a white, brown, or palomino base coat. In England, pinto is also called colored or odd-colored. A piebald is a black-and-white pinto. A skewbald is a brown-and-white pinto.

When we talk about colors versus color breeds, we use different rules of capitalization. We capitalize a registered breed name, but not a color name.

> The United States has two primary breeds for pinto-colored horses: Pinto and Paint. The Pinto registry is open to horses of any breed that exhibit pinto coloring. The Paint registry is open only to horses with at least one parent who is registered Paint. The other parent must be a registered Paint, Thoroughbred, or Quarter Horse. This includes solid-colored horses! Therefore, you can have a Pinto who is not a Paint, or a Paint who is not a pinto!

Appaloosas have smaller spots than pintos. A leopard Appaloosa has a white or light-colored coat covered with dark spots. A blanket Appaloosa has white over her back and haunches. Often the white patch will have spots the color of the rest of the base coat. A snowflake Appaloosa has white or light spots throughout a dark-colored base coat. Some Appaloosas are born solid-colored and remain that way through life. They can still pass on the colored markings to their foals.

Quirky Colors

Some horses pass on genes that modify the horse's base color. Gray is the most common. Gray foals will be born the color that their base color genes dictate. In most cases that's black or brown. Over time, the gray gene works to change that coat color to gray, or even pure white!

> The Lipizzaner breed is a famous example of a gray breed. Rarely, bay or black foals stay the color they were at birth throughout their life. They are considered lucky!

Grays can be solid, flea-bitten (speckled), or dappled (covered with round spots slightly darker than the base coat). Gray horses are prone to develop melanoma as they age. Melanoma is a type of skin cancer. It often appears

as lumps under a horse's tail. In most cases, melanoma is not harmful or painful.

The Dilution Solution

Some genes cause the base coat to appear lighter. We call these dilutions. Common dilute colors are:

- **Palomino:** creamy or gold base coat, with white mane and tail
- **Cremello:** very light cream base coat with blue eyes
- **Champagne:** cream with chocolate points
- **Buckskin:** tan with dark points
- **Dun:** tan with dark points, a dark stripe down the back (dorsal stripe) and often stripes on the legs
- **Grullo:** dark gray with the dorsal and leg stripes

Add-On Identifiers

A brand is a design burned into the skin to identify the owner or breed. It usually remains hairless. A freeze brand is a brand made by freezing instead of burning. The hair on a freeze brand often grows back white. Often it is located along the neck, below the mane. Standardbreds and mustangs receive freeze brands.

Thoroughbreds and Quarter Horses traditionally received tattoos on the inside of their upper lip before they begin racing to identify exactly who they are. They are now microchipped instead. You may still see lip tattoos on older horses.

MARKED FOR GREATNESS

Markings are white patches that make each horse unique. They can show up on any colored coat. Think of markings like sprinkles on ice cream!

Markings on the Head

- Star: a mark on the forehead
- Stripe: a narrow marking down the face
- Blaze: a wide marking down the face
- Bald face: a wide blaze that may go beyond the eyes.
- Snip: a mark on the muzzle

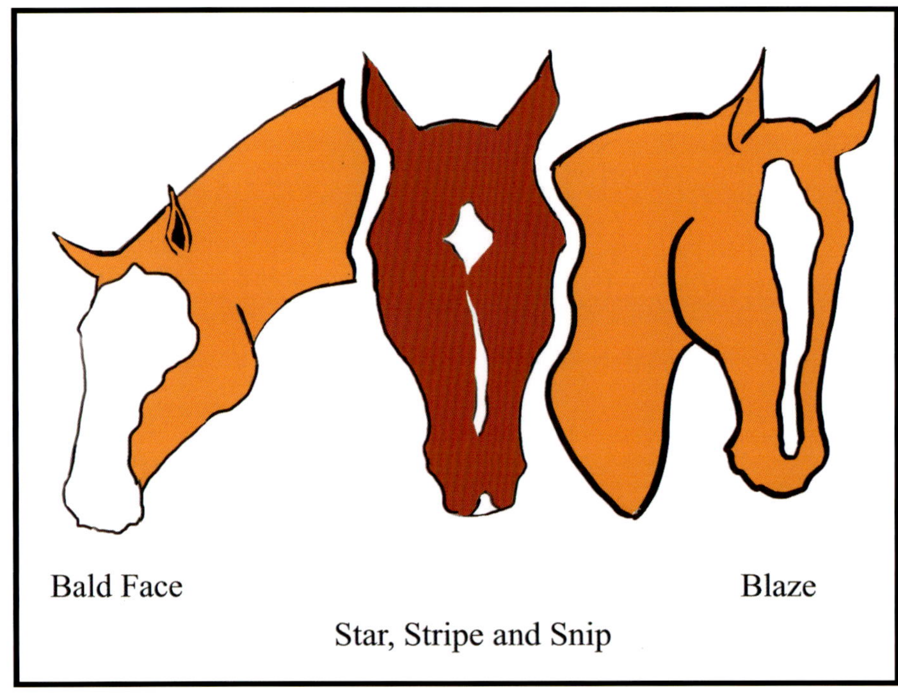

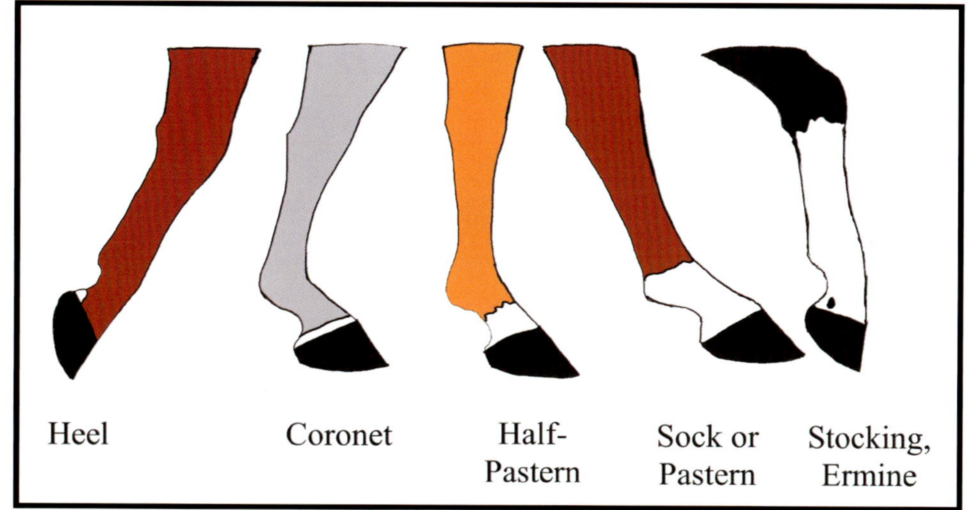

Markings on the Legs

- Coronet: a white band just above the hoof
- Heel spot: a white spot on the heel
- Half-pastern: white from hoof halfway up the pastern
- Sock: white from hoof to above the fetlock
- Stocking: white from hoof to knee
- Ermine spots: dark spots on white markings

A scar is the result of an old injury. The hair on a scar often grows in white, or doesn't grow back at all. Scars can tell a story of the horse's history. White flecks across the bridge of the nose tell of a halter adjusted too tight or left on too long. White patches or a white tuft of mane on the horse's withers tell of a badly fitting saddle, saddle pad, or blanket.

Strange Spots

"Birdcatcher spots" are named after a famous Irish Thoroughbred foaled in 1833. They are white dots that show up on an otherwise solid coat, often after the horse has matured. Sometimes they disappear or show up in new places. Some scientists think they are genetic while others think they are a sign of a nutritional deficiency. Nobody knows for sure!

> Birdcatcher and Bend Or are horses that are remembered for their spots. Does your favorite horse have a unique marking, color, or personality trait? Invent a name for it that will be remembered forever!

"Bend Or spots" are named after another famous Thoroughbred stallion foaled in England in 1877. These dark marks are found on palominos and chestnuts. Like Birdcatcher spots, they usually appear as the horse matures.

"Ink spots," common in pintos, are dark spots inside a larger white patch. They are also called "cat tracks" or "paw prints."

Horses on the Inside

Just like us, horses are held up by a bony skeleton. Muscles, tendons, and ligaments help that skeleton move around. Organs such as the heart, lungs, and stomach perform the vital functions that keep the horse alive. All of these structures work together to keep horses healthy and happy.

When something goes wrong with any part of the horse, he becomes sick. Some illnesses and injuries can be treated easily. Some require extensive treatment. If you are ever in doubt, ask a knowledgeable adult, or call your veterinarian.

If the horse's skeleton, muscles, tendons, or ligaments, become injured, we call him lame, or unsound. A lame horse may move differently on the injured leg or nod his head when he moves.

Sometimes we can see an injury or swelling. Sometimes we can feel extra heat in the injured part. This is why it is so important to know how your horse's legs normally feel as well as how they look.

Problems usually start small and grow slowly. The closer attention you pay to how your horse looks and feels, the sooner you will notice if something is not quite right. If a problem is caught and treated early on, it has a better chance for a good outcome.

Make a daily habit of using your eyes and your hands to go over your entire horse. It is easy to include this in your grooming routine. Learn what looks and feels normal so you immediately recognize when something is a little off. Learn to

HORSE FEEDING FUNDAMENTALS

Horses are special animals, and they need the right kind of food to stay happy and healthy. Horses mostly eat grass and hay (dried grass). They also get horse food called grain or pellets for extra energy. They love healthy treats like apples and carrots, but just like candy for us, too many treats can be bad!

Horses' digestive organs are very similar to ours, but there are three major differences: the teeth, the stomach, and the cecum (SEE-kum). These differences show us why it is so important to follow rules for feeding horses.

Remember our friends Mesohippus and Merychippus from horse history? Their teeth grew larger and more in number. They could chew tough grasses and twigs. Because they were constantly nibbling on the fields and forests around them, their stomachs are smaller than yours and mine. That means a big meal can make them sick or even kill them.

Horses evolved an extra organ in their digestive system called the cecum. The cecum is a huge pouch between the small and large intestines. It is almost four feet long. The cecum is filled with good bacteria, which are able to break down hay and grass into nutrients. Any big changes in what we feed horses can kill the good bacteria and make the horse sick. Because humans do not have a cecum, we cannot eat hay and grass to survive.

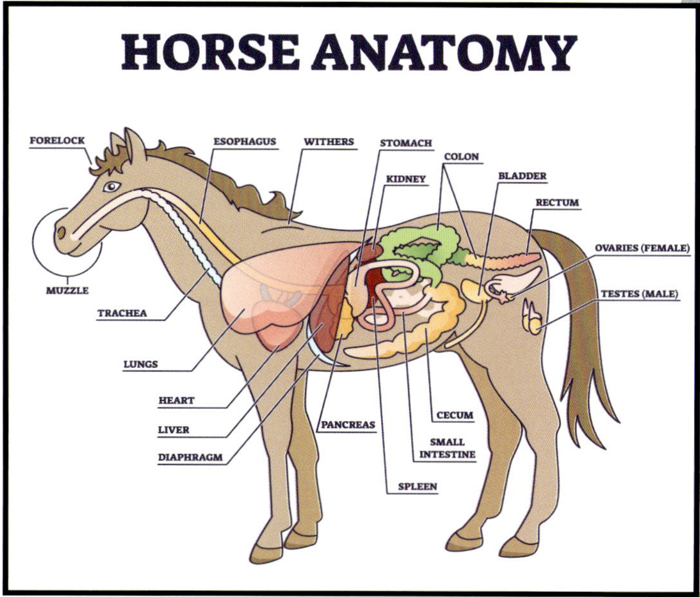

Top 10 Rules of Feeding

1. Feed small amounts often. Horses' stomachs are small for their size.
2. Have a regular feed routine. Horses love routine!
3. Provide fresh, clean water at all times.
4. Provide a source of salt and minerals at all times.
5. Feed plenty of good quality hay, free from mold, dust, or weeds.
6. Feed according to your horse's weight and workload.
7. Make any changes slowly to help the good bacteria adjust.
8. Keep feed scoops and buckets clean. No one like to eat on dirty dishes!
9. Watch your horse's weight and condition. Adjust the feed as needed.
10. Talk to your vet and instructor to make the healthiest menu for your horse.

take the horse's vital signs. If anything is out of the ordinary, ask for help.

Vital Signs

Vital signs are measurements that tell us how healthy a horse is. These numbers can tell us if she is sick or let us treat an illness before it becomes more serious. They can help a veterinarian identify exactly what is wrong.

There are three main signs we examine: temperature, pulse, and respiration. If you think of them together as "TPR," you will remember them easily.

Temperature

Temperature measures how warm or cool your horse's body is. Just as humans sometimes run fevers when they are ill, a horse's temperature will often increase when he is sick. Normal equine temperature is 99–101 degrees Fahrenheit (37–38 degrees Celsius). We measure temperature by inserting a thermometer into the horse's anus (bottom).

Top Tip: Horses may have a higher or lower normal temperature. Temperature may also change slightly throughout the day. While the horse is healthy, take their temperature several days in a row, at the same time each day. Consider the average as the normal temperature. Why is this important? If your horse's normal is 99, then a temperature of 101, even though it is still considered normal, tells you she might be getting sick.

Pulse

Pulse refers to your horse's heartbeat. A normal pulse is between 28 and 44 beats per minute. You can hear the pulse through a stethoscope or feel it in an artery (blood vessel) under the horse's jaw. A pulse can be tricky to feel at first. Practice counting the beats carefully while the horse is healthy, so you know how to measure it when you think he is sick.

Top Tip: Sometimes your horse gets antsy if you count for a full minute. You can also count for fifteen seconds and multiply that number by four.

Respiration

Respiration measures the number of breaths a horse takes in a minute. Normal respiration is between eight and sixteen full breaths. Respiration is easy to count if you watch the horse's flanks or nostrils as he inhales and exhales.

Top Tip: If you can't see the exhalations, hold the back of your hand close to the nostrils to feel for breath.

Healthy as a Horse

A healthy horse looks bright and shiny. She is alert and interested. She doesn't show any wounds or unusual swellings. She is not favoring a leg (though she may rest a hind leg when she is relaxed). Her vital signs are normal. She has no difficulty eating, drinking, pooping or peeing.

Sometimes you have a feeling your horse is not quite right, even if you do not see anything obviously wrong. Perhaps a normally curious horse seems disinterested or listless. Maybe she is laying down for a nap at an unusual time. Anything out of the ordinary invites you to look more carefully and keep a close watch.

When things go wrong, always talk to a knowledgeable adult. Together you can decide if you want to call your veterinarian. As a team, you can treat the problem and return your horse to health.

TOP TEN SIGNS OF SICKNESS

- Visible injuries or lameness
- Signs of belly pain ("colic"), including refusing to eat, biting or kicking at her sides, rolling, getting up and down, sweating, or stretching out
- Cloudy, swollen, or injured eye
- Coughing
- Runny eyes or nose, especially if cloudy or colored
- Changes in manure, such as diarrhea, excessively dry manure, straining, or changes in frequency
- Depressed or cranky, either on the ground or while riding
- Changes in vital signs (fever, panting, high heart rate, or excessively low measurements)
- Signs of "choke," including nasal discharge, slobbering, gagging, pawing, and straining to swallow
- Rapid changes in weight

Routine Health Care

Just like you go to the doctor and dentist for regular check-ups, your horse does too. He will need vaccinations, or shots, at least once a year. He will need his teeth "floated," or filed.

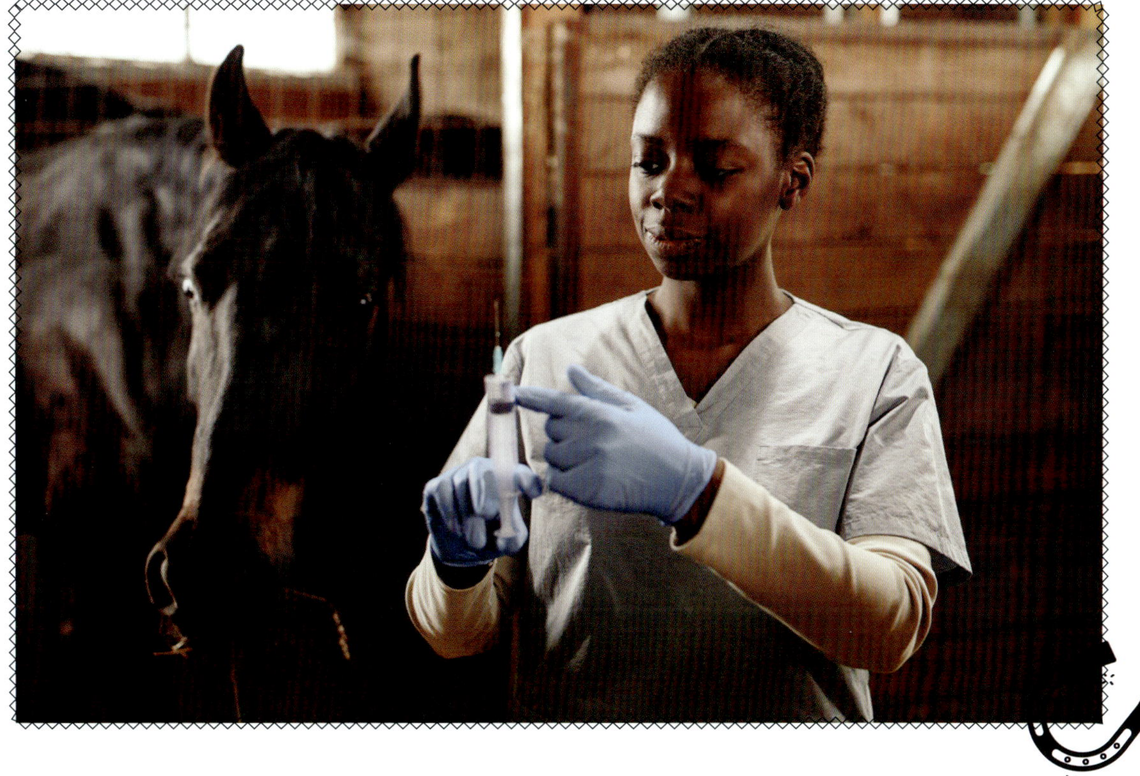

Your horse requires deworming to kill internal parasites, or worms. Your vet and instructor will help you determine how often and with which products. Recommendations change as parasites develop resistance to available drugs, and researchers make new discoveries. All the animals in your horse's turnout group need to be dewormed at the same time to prevent reinfestation.

Your horse will need trims or shoeing with his farrier (blacksmith) around every 6–8 weeks. Horses in hard work or healing from injuries may also need treatment from professionals such as chiropractors or acupuncturists.

Keep track of appointments in your horse journal. Include questions you want to remember to ask your horse's health team the next time you see them. Write down new information you learn. Illustrate your entries with photographs and drawings.

4

Horses . . . Naturally!

The best way to learn about people's nature, thoughts, and actions is to watch them with their friends and families. Learning about horses is the same! In chapter 2, you learned who is whom in the herd. Now let's step into a group of horses, called a band or a herd, to learn more about horses . . . naturally!

Who Are the People in Your Neighborhood?

Horses are very social creatures. Their survival depends on their neighbors (or should we call them "neigh"-bors!?). A lone horse in the wild might soon be eaten by predators. When a horse is part of a larger group, everyone can team up to find food, keep watch, and fight hungry enemies.

A family band is usually made up of a stallion, one or more mares, and their young offspring. As the stallion's sons (and often daughters) approach maturity, he will chase them out of the band. The fillies will join another stallion's band. A colt will join a bachelor band or try to create his own band of mares.

A bachelor band is made up of the young stallions that have been chased out of their family bands. Together they defend against predators and play-fight each other. Play-fighting builds their fitness and teaches them other stallions' weaknesses. As the colts gain strength, smarts, and survival skills, they will try to steal mares from other stallions to create their own family bands.

How can a stallion steal a mare? Sometimes a mare wanders too far from her band. A watchful rival stallion will race in and chase her to his own band. Sometimes he is fast enough to succeed. If the other stallion notices and chases him down, he needs to decide if the new mare is worth fighting for.

Stallion fights can be vicious. Their teeth are strong. Their hooves are sharp and their kicks are powerful enough to break bone. A horse can die immediately from their fight wounds, or later from infection or broken bones. As older stallions lose strength and speed, younger stallions will challenge them more often.

A "band" of horses is the proper term for a small group of horses that stick together. Usually a band consists of a family: a stallion, a group of mares, and their foals. It can also mean a group of friends whose instincts have brought them together to find food and fight predators. The word "herd" refers to all of the bands within a larger area. Despite the distinctions, the two words are often used interchangeably.

A stallion's main jobs are to help defend his mares from threats, to breed, and to steal more

mares for his band. The day-to-day decisions are usually left to one or more lead mares. She (or they) will decide when to visit the watering hole or move on to new foraging grounds.

Mares also help protect the herd from predators. Running is always their first instinct. But if they are trapped, mares will circle around the defenseless foals to fight off enemies.

"Snaking" refers to a horse lowering his head with his teeth bared and ears flattened back, looking like a snake about to attack another horse. The stallion will follow up with sharp bites if he is ignored. Both mares and stallions will "snake" bandmates they want to dominate.

Horses form strong social bonds. We might even call them friendships. They may graze together, groom each other with gentle nibbles, or swish flies off their friend's face with their tails. They may care for or discipline each other's foals.

Pecking Order

Horses know their survival depends on their community. They also know where they rank in the band. This ranking is called the "pecking order" because it is also seen in chickens. Chickens peck the others in their flock to gain status.

How do horses show their confidence and strength in the pecking order? They exhibit good leadership in the band. If they are challenged, they show off with body language, arching their necks, pinning their ears back, pawing the ground, or "snaking." Sometimes they resort to fighting with kicks, bites, and body slams.

Most horses would rather avoid a fight. They know where they stand in the pecking order, and do not challenge the stronger, bossier horses who rank above them. They know their survival could depend on being a member of the group, even if it is a low rank. This acceptance of leadership helps us work with horses. If they trust that we are a fair leader, they are happy to follow.

The pecking order is a natural part of a band's social behavior. Even the quietest horse may act "wild" when he meets a new horse, especially when he feels threatened. Keep this in mind when introducing unfamiliar horses and keep yourself safe!

How Horses Sense

Like humans, horses take in the world around them through their senses. The five senses are sight, hearing, touch, smell, and taste. Their senses are often sharper than ours, so they see and hear things that we may not. You learned that horses have

OBSERVING HORSE BEHAVIOR

Experts are still learning how to decode equine intelligence and behavior. Once, they believed the lead stallion made all the decisions. Then they thought that a lead mare was usually in charge. Now they realize that decisions that affect the band might be made by several individuals. They all agree that we can keep learning by carefully observing the horses themselves.

How can you become an equine behaviorist? Ask your instructor if there is a safe place where you can watch a group of horses interacting naturally in a paddock or pasture. Quiet the part of your brain that automatically tries to give answers and pay attention to what you are actually seeing. Use your senses of vision, hearing, touch, and smell. Capture your thoughts in your horse journal.

evolved with the constant threat of being eaten by predators. The sharper their senses, the sooner they know to run to safety!

Eye Spy

Look carefully at your horse's face. Notice how the eyes are set off to the sides of the forehead. This is typical of a prey animal (an animal that is eaten by predators). The horse has a wide range of vision that can include the entire environment, except what is directly behind, in front, or beneath his head. This includes obstacles and even jumps.

> Once he gets close, a horse cannot clearly see the jump he is being asked to clear!

The Nose Knows

Horses have an extraordinary sense of smell. They have up to sixty times as many "olfactory receptors" (the cells that detect smells) as humans. They also have a special structure in the roof of their mouth called a "vomeronasal organ" (voh-mer-oh-NAY-sal), which increases their ability to smell more.

Smells tell horses what is tasty or unsafe to eat, if a mare is ready to breed, and even help identify other horses and humans. Smells can signal a threat or a predator. Many horses are more alert or anxious on windy days, because of scents carried by the breeze.

Sometimes you will see a horse lift his head and curl his lip up after smelling something. This is called the Flehmen (FLAY-man) response. It may look like the horse is laughing. This allows scent to go directly to the vomeronasal organ to be better understood.

Do You Hear What I Hear?

Horses' ears are large, expressive, and almost constantly moving. You can tell where a horse's attention is focused by where his ears are pointing.

Equine ears can swivel almost 180 degrees. They act like moveable "funnels" to catch even the smallest sounds and send them through the ear canal to the brain. Each ear can move independently. Horses can change their range of hearing by lifting, lowering, or tilting their heads. Horses can hear a much broader range of frequencies than humans.

HUMANS HELPING HORSES

Dr. Jordan saves foals' lives using the power of smell.

"A magical moment that I've helped with several times has been "grafting" a mare and orphan foal who aren't related so that they become a bonded pair. We give the mare special medications. We rub Vicks VapoRub on the mare's muzzle and on the foal. The peppermint smell masks the foal's own smell, and makes the mare think the baby is hers! The mare adopts the baby! I love seeing them grazing in the field together."

JUST SAY NEIGH

Horses' spoken language is an important way they communicate. Their vocalizations include:

- **Nicker:** a soft, vibrating sound that communicates a friendly greeting. Horses may nicker to their friends, foals, and favorite people. Nickering can also mean anticipation of feed, treats, or other positive things.
- **Neigh:** a loud, high-pitched sound that can carry over long distances. Neighing broadcasts excitement, concern, or calling for attention. Often horses will neigh when they are separated from their friends.
- **Whinny:** similar to a neigh, but softer and more musical. Whinnies mean much the same as nickers. Some people use the word interchangeably with neigh.
- **Squeal:** high-pitched sound that communicates dominance, discomfort, interest, or anger.
- **Snort:** a sharp, loud exhale used to express concern, danger, or aggression.
- **Blow:** similar to a snort but softer and longer lasting. Blowing communicates relaxation and acceptance.
- **Groan:** a long, low-pitched moan that admits discomfort, pain, and distress.

In Good Taste

A horse's sense of taste evolved to help them identify edible food. Taste can identify poisonous plants and nourishing vegetation. Taste can help horses avoid a deadly meal.

Taste preferences can be very personal. Horses may prefer some feeds to others. Usually they enjoy sweet flavors, so molasses is often added to grain to tempt a picky eater. The smart trainer notices a horse's favorite tastes and uses those as a reward for a job well done.

Touchy Feely

Horses rely heavily on the sense of touch. They explore their environment with their muzzles, gathering crucial information. They may nudge other animals to communicate. They use their lips and teeth (gently!) to bond through grooming each other.

Horses can feel vibrations through their hooves and jawbones as well as their skin. This allows them to "hear" things around them in ways that most humans do not.

The horse's sense of touch lets us communicate through the pressure of the reins, legs, and weight. Horses are sensitive enough to feel a fly land on their skin. They are able to feel and respond to even tiny shifts in the rider's balance and posture.

Like cats and dogs, horses have whiskers around their muzzles and eyes. Whisker hair, called vibrissae (vih-BRIH-see or vie-BRIH-see), is different than regular hair. It is long and stiff. Each whisker is deeply rooted and has many more

nerve endings than regular hair. These nerve endings send information to the brain about what the whiskers are sensing.

Remember that horses cannot see directly in front of them. Whiskers can let the horse "see" through what they feel. The whiskers on their muzzle also help them identify which plants are tasty to eat and which are harmful or inedible like rocks.

Whiskers used to be shaved off to provide a "cleaner" look. The Fedération Equestre International (FEI), which makes rules for horse sports around the world, passed a law in 2020 making it illegal to shave horses' whiskers. Though local horse shows may not have to follow those rules, thoughtful horsemen often choose to let their horse's whiskers grow as long and as useful as nature intended.

Sense and Sensibility

Now you have a better idea of how horses experience the world. They sense sounds, sights, and smells that we do not. Their instinct as a prey animal is to run away from anything unfamiliar that might be a threat, or to fight if they feel trapped.

> Think about when you saw a horse act up or "misbehave." What do you think the wild part of his brain was saying?

When a horse acts up, they may be responding to something outside of human awareness. The sensible horseman realizes this. Let horses inspire you to sharpen your own senses!

5

Horse Whispering

Throughout time there have been trainers who were so tuned in to horses that they were able to achieve amazing results without any visible efforts. These came to be known as "horse whisperers" for their special way of communicating with horses. While some were cheaters and fakes, others really did have an almost magical skill.

We now know that these talented trainers deeply understood a horse's nature and behavior. They could clearly "read" the horse's body language. They could respond with their own body language in such a way that horses could easily understand.

In the last chapter, you learned about how horses think, behave, and vocalize with each other. In this chapter, you will learn to think, behave, and communicate with your horse. Developing this degree of skill with horses requires patience, training, and tons of practice. Horsemen never stop learning!

Overcoming Instinct

Horses survived millions of years of evolution thanks to their instincts. Their innate urges are to flee from danger, to fight when trapped, and to form a strong community (band or herd) to increase chances of survival.

Good horsemen know this. They recognize when environments or situations might trigger these instincts. They help the horse learn to overcome instinct.

Through a careful, step-by-step process, trainers desensitize horses to threats, teach them to trust, and train them to respond to aids—another word horsemen use for cues. Each step forward is small and understandable, which makes it easier for the horse to learn. When horses have difficulty learning, good trainers will create even smaller steps. This is called "chunking down."

Pressure, Release, and Reward

Horses learn through pressure and release. Pressure is just another word for a cue. It might be a physical pressure such as a steady touch of hand, leg, or rein. It might be a suggested pressure, such as the visual presence of body language, a whip, or a twirling lead rope. Pressure should not cause pain.

The horse notices when the pressure is released. He will associate what he was doing with the removal of the pressure and tend to repeat it. The trainer is responsible for perfectly timing the release of pressure with the desired behavior.

Reward goes beyond release of pressure. Reward is offering something enjoyable for the desired behavior. This could be a soft pat or scratch on the horse's favorite itchy spot, a spoken "good boy," or a treat. As with the release of pressure, timing the reward to the behavior is everything.

Let's look at a common case. A horse is learning to canter with a rider. The trainer cannot feed a treat at the moment of the transition. She would need to bring the horse back down to the walk or halt. By then, the horse would associate the reward with the last thing that happened. In this case, that would be the halt rather than the canter transition. The trainer needs to remove the pressure (stop the leg

> Clicker training, also called "operant conditioning," is a reward-based training system. The horse is taught to associate the sound of a "click," either from a hand-held mechanism or from the trainer's voice, with a reward. This allows the trainer to mark the exact moment the desired behavior happened, even if they cannot offer the reward just then. Because the horse has learned that the click marks "good job, right now," he knows what the reward is for, even if it takes a few seconds to get the treat.

or vocal cue) and offer the reward (a "good boy," or a pet) the moment the horse picked up canter for the horse to make the connection.

From a Whisper to a Shout

Imagine your mom asks you to clean your room. If you ignore her, she might ask again, loudly and firmly. If you keep ignoring her, she might shout at you or threaten to punish you.

Now, imagine that she didn't ask you nicely first. What if she just started yelling and screaming? How would that make you feel?

When you give an aid or a cue, ask first as lightly as possible. This trains the horse to "listen for a whisper." If you always use strong, yelled commands, your horse will learn to ignore everything but the shouts. This is no fun for either of you!

> Most of the time, horses try to do the right thing. If the horse is not responding to your aids, check in with yourself. Are you applying the aids correctly? Are you unconsciously blocking the horse with a conflicting aid (for example, asking for a canter but pulling on the reins)? Are you asking for something the horse has not yet learned how to do?

If the horse does not respond to a light cue and you are certain that you asked him correctly, apply the aid more strongly until you get a response. Praise the horse immediately, then repeat the request, once again using the lightest of aids.

BODY LANGUAGE

Horses communicate through silent body language. They hold entire conversations with their posture and expressions. When you learn how to "read" this language, you are on your way to speaking horse!

Head

- A raised head indicates excitement, interest, or aggression.
- A low head conveys relaxation, exhaustion, illness, or submission.
- Wrinkles around the mouth, nostrils, and eyes communicates anxiety, anger, or fear.

Eyes

- Eyes rolled back, showing white, communicates anger or fear.
- Wrinkles around the eyes can indicate anxiety.
- Wide, soft eyes suggest contentment.

Ears

- Ears pinned back communicates anger or aggression. Sometimes a horse will flick his ears back to focus on his rider.
- Ears pricked forward shows where horses are focusing or expresses excitement, anticipation, or curiosity.
- Ears held neutral conveys relaxation or contentment. If a horse is moving, her ears might flop in rhythm with her paces.

Mouth

- Gentle nibbles usually indicate friendliness or playfulness. Sometimes horses will attempt to nibble you while being groomed, as part of their instinct to groom their friends.
- Biting communicates dominance, aggression, or pain.
- Licking and softly chewing conveys release of tension, relaxation, or submission.
- Teeth "clacking," also called "baby talk" because we see young foals do it with dominant horses, says, "I'm no threat to you—please leave me alone!"

Hooves

- Pawing or wall-kicking can indicate boredom, annoyance, or discomfort.
- A single stomp, particularly when meeting a new horse, conveys dominance or aggression.

- A kick can communicate playfulness, aggression, pain, or feeling threatened.

Tail

- A low, relaxed, swinging tail tells us the horse is contented.
- A tail carried high ("flagged") conveys excitement.
- A rapidly swishing tail communicates annoyance and anxiety, and it may be a warning that a kick is coming.
- A tail held to the side suggests a mare might be interested in breeding.

No Means No! Or Does It . . .

Animal behavior experts agree is that it is far more difficult for an animal to understand a negative than a positive. In other words, it is more difficult to understand commands like no, quit, or don't than a request for a different behavior. For example, imagine your horse is jigging and prancing when you would like a calm walk. Instead of saying "no" or "quit," calm your energy and ask for slower steps.

Horses use their energy levels as well as body language to communicate. You can learn to control and direct your focus and energy to communicate with horses too, just like learning any other skill.

Imagine how it feels to be reading a book or watching TV. How does that feel in your body? When the scene you're reading or watching gets really exciting, or intense, or scary, what happens to your energy level? Can you quiet it back down again? You can, with practice.

Once you get the hang of raising or lowering your energy, practice in the real world. Most kids find it pretty easy to raise their energy when things are calm, but with horses, we need to practice lowering our energy when things get exciting or scary. When you are in a tense or exciting situation, relax your body, breathe deeply, and lower your energy. Try doing this the next time you talk to someone who is upset or angry. These efforts can help calm people too!

An Alphabet of Aids

"Aids" are the signals we use to communicate with our horse. They are also called cues. Think of aids like an alphabet: they can be put together, like letters, to make more complicated words and sentences to talk with a horse.

Natural Aids

Natural aids are a part of you. These include your energy, voice, legs, hands, and seat/body. Your energy is a powerful communicator. The horse will often tune-in and respond to your energy, even when you are unaware of it.

- Calming your energy will help both you and your horse to relax and focus.
- Increasing your energy can create impulsion in a lazy horse or upset a sensitive steed.
- Focusing intently or "sending" your energy can give your horse clear direction.

Our **voices** can communicate direction and emotion. Horses do not speak English naturally, but they can learn some vocabulary. Tone of voice is even more important than the words spoken. The voice can also help the human to relax or focus.

- To settle a nervous horse, speak in a low, slow, calm tone.
- To ask for an upward transition (increase of speed), use an energetic tone of voice that rises on the second syllable, like "walk ON" or "canTER." You can also make a kissing or clucking sound.

"Horse sense" means sound, practical knowledge, or common sense. The expression was first used in 1832. No one knows if the phrase is based on horses themselves, or the characteristics of people who work with horses successfully. Maybe it is a little of both!

- To ask a horse to slow or stop, speak in a low, confident voice that deepens on the second syllable, like "AND whoa."
- Voice cues must be consistent. Each word should have only one meaning. For example, "whoa" means "stop" every time, and not "slow down" or "steady."

Legs give a brief squeeze in specific places.

- Both legs at the girth says, "move faster."
- One leg at the girth signals "bend your body." It can also block sideways movement.

- One leg behind the girth means “move your hindquarters over,” “canter,” or “stop moving your hindquarters over.”
- Both legs behind the girth sometimes means “back up.”

Hands squeeze the reins, like you are wringing water out of a sponge, then soften their grip without opening your fingers or letting go.

- One hand, especially when moved away from the horse’s neck, says “turn in this direction.” This is called an opening or leading rein.
- Both hands mean “slow down” or “stop.”
- One hand used towards the horse’s neck signals “turn towards the opposite direction.” This is the foundation of one-handed Western riding. It can also mean “stop moving sideways.”

Body position and **weight** are powerful aids both on the ground and in the saddle. Remember, horses are so sensitive they can feel a fly land anywhere on their skin, so they feel any changes in their riders’ bodies.

- Looking where you want to go tells your horse whether you want him to go straight or turn. Your head can weigh more than ten pounds, so your horse can feel where you are looking.

- Rotating your body from your seat to your shoulders tells your horse what direction you want to go. Imagine a flashlight shining out of your belly button, lighting the way.
- Stretching tall and squeezing your shoulders back can mean "slow down" or "stop." It can also mean "pay attention" or "get balanced."

Notice how the natural aids can ask for different responses. When aids are used in various combinations, they have distinct meanings. When you are an absolute beginner, you will learn the simplest aids to direct your horse. As your knowledge and skills grow, you will learn more complex and subtle ways to communicate more clearly.

Artificial Aids

Artificial aids are man-made tools such as spurs, whips, crops (short whips), and specialized bits, nosebands, and martingales or tie-downs. They reinforce the action of natural aids. They should only be used as follow-up when the horse ignores the natural aid.

Artificial aids should be used as lightly as possible to get a response. They should never be used as punishment. The rider must be sure they have an independent seat and are using their natural aids correctly before turning to artificial aids.

REAL HORSES, REAL RIDERS

Tina and Kevin are both talented riders. They board at the same stable. One day, they thought it would be fun to teach Kevin's pony Frolic how to rear. Frolic was smart and learned quickly. Soon she would eagerly rear on cue. Tina and Kevin had great fun, and probably learned a lot about training horses. But let's look what happened later on.When Kevin outgrew his beloved pony, Frolic was sold to Bree, a timid child who was just learning to ride. The well-trained Frolic seemed to be a perfect match. But one day Bree accidentally gave Frolic the cue to rear. Up reared Frolic, off tumbled Bree!

In Frolic's mind, she was doing what she was told. In Bree's mind, this was a very scary fall that destroyed her shaky trust in her pony. A trainer who was not aware of Frolic's previous training might actually punish the pony, even though she was responding correctly to a cue.

As you improve in your horsemanship, you will have the skills to teach horses more and more. But with the skills comes responsibility: you can, but should you? Always keep your horse's best interests, both today and in the future, foremost in your mind!

6

Every Day with Horses

Now that you know how to understand and talk to horses, let's learn how to take care of them!

Horses thrive on routine. They have excellent memories, and they gain confidence when they know what to expect next. Routines also help you remember to do everything that needs to be done and decrease the chance that you will forget something important. We will now go through a typical daily routine.

Approaching a Horse

1. Walk towards the horse's shoulder. If you walk towards his face or his haunches, he may feel that as a cue to move away. Rub his shoulder and lay the lead rope over his neck. This way, if he moves off, you quickly grab the other end and keep control.

2. Holding the halter's crownpiece in your right hand, put your arm over his neck. Slip the noseband over his muzzle and buckle or tie the crownpiece.
3. Hold the lead rope with your right hand about six inches down from the halter. Fold the rest of the rope in your left hand. Never coil the rope around your hand. If your horse were to get startled and pull, you could break a bone.
4. Stand beside your horse's neck and ask him to walk on with a cluck, a kiss, or a verbal cue.

HOW TO TIE A ROPE HALTER

Slide the crownpiece through the tie loop from back to front. Bring the crown piece to the right, then behind the loop towards the front. Finish by tucking the end through the loop you just formed. Pull the knot snug.

Many novices make the mistake of tying the knot around the crownpiece rather than the tie knot. This can make the knot difficult or impossible to remove.

Never leave the horse unattended when he is wearing a rope halter, which will not break under pressure. In an emergency, a rope halter could cause severe injury or even death. Instead, use a leather or breakaway halter for turnout or everyday use.

Clean Your Room!

How many times do we hear that from our parents? Cleaning your horse's room is even more important. A clean stall keeps bugs away, stops stinky smells, and keeps your horse's hooves, coat, and lungs healthy.

While it is natural and healthy for horses to live in a safe pasture with shelter full-time, most horses live part-time in stalls. Even if your horse lives at a boarding stable, a good horseman knows how to clean stalls. It's easy once you get the hang of it!

1. Gather your tools: a pitchfork or manure fork, a wheelbarrow or muck tub, and a broom.
2. Use your pitchfork to pick up all the manure (horse poop) and dump it into the wheelbarrow.
3. Find the wet spots in the shavings or straw, and scoop those out.
4. If the bedding (shavings or straw) is still clean and dry, shake it out with your fork and leave it in the stall.
5. Add fresh bedding so your horse has a soft, dry place to stand and lie down.
6. Scrub the water bucket and refill with fresh water
7. Sweep the front of the stall and tidy things up so it looks neat.
8. Dump the wheelbarrow in the manure pile or compost area.

Ties and Cross-ties

If you are going to groom and tack your horse, you will secure him to prevent him from wandering away.

Horses should always be tied with a quick-release knot to prevent accidents or injuries. If he panics and you need to release him in a hurry, simply pull the end of the rope. There are several types of quick release knots. Your instructor and vet will show you their favorite. See how many different quick release knots you can learn! Track them in your horse journal.

Many barns have cross-ties in the aisles. Ropes from the walls are clipped to each side of the halter. Often, they will have special breakaway snaps in case of an emergency.

SAFE HORSE HANDLING

- Always act calm. Do not make sudden noises or movements.
- Be aware of your environment. Things that seem ordinary to you may seem alarming to your horse.
- Be aware of your horse's body language. If he seems anxious or upset, try to identify the stressor and remove it.
- Be aware of your horse's blind spots. You learned in chapter 3 that your horse cannot see directly in front of or behind him. He will be more likely to be startled by noises or movements in these areas.
- Be aware of your horse's feet. He may step on you if you are not paying attention.

Grooming

Grooming is important for many reasons. It is vital to your horse's health. Dirt trapped under tack can cause discomfort and sores. Grooming increases bonding and strengthens your relationship. A good grooming routine lets you thoroughly check your horse's body to see if anything is out of the ordinary, such as wounds or swelling. Best of all, done right, grooming makes your horse feel great!

1. Pick your horse's hooves. Hold the hoof pick in your right hand, with the pick by your pinky. This is the opposite of how most people want to hold it instinctively, but it will give you more strength and control.
2. Stand next to your horse's shoulder, facing toward his tail with your feet parallel to his belly. This keeps your feet out of the way if your horse stomps unexpectedly. Slide your hand down your horse's leg and pick up his hoof. Work from the heels towards the toe, digging out any dirt or rocks. Work carefully around the heels and frog, which can be sensitive.

3. Use a mane brush or human hairbrush to detangle the horse's mane and tail and brush the underlying skin.

Tail hair grows slowly, so consider using a detangling product before brushing, or brush it less frequently. Some horsemen even pick the tangles out carefully by hand to avoid breaking or thinning the tail hairs.

4. Use the rubber curry in a circular motion to loosen hair and caked on dirt. Currying is also a great massage! Avoid the head or legs with anything but the softest curries. Rough action with a stiff curry could bruise these bony parts.
5. Using a stiff brush or dandy brush in the direction of your horse's coat, remove the dirt and hair loosened by the curry. Remember to change the direction of the strokes where the hair swirls backwards along your horse's flanks.

6. Use a soft brush or body brush to clean all the way down to the skin, and to put a shine on your horse's coat. Use a towel or rub a rag all over your horse's body for a final polish.

Saddling

1. Make sure the underside of the saddle pad is clean. Dirt can cause a rub, and a stuck burr can cause bucking!

2. Place the pad on the horses back several inches ahead of the withers, then slide it into place so the horses fur lies flat. If you start too far back and pull the pad forward, the hairs will be pulled and trapped, causing discomfort.
3. Place the saddle on your horse's back. "Peak" your pad. This means pull it into the pommel of your saddle so there is plenty of clearance for your horse's withers. Forgetting this can cause bad behavior or a nasty sore!
4. Fasten the girth to the first and third billet, making sure they are on the same hole. Buckle the other side of the girth. Adjust it just snugly enough to stabilize the saddle. Make sure the buckles are about the same height on either side. A western girth, called a cinch, fastens onto a single latigo strap with either a buckle or a knot.
5. You will tighten the girth gradually until it is time to mount. Rushing this can make the horse "cold-backed." She might let you know her discomfort by biting, kicking, or bucking.

LET'S TALK TACK

Different riding styles use different tack, the name we use for riding gear. Tack usually includes a bridle and saddle that are designed to help with the job at hand. For example, western saddles have a "horn" on the front to tie off a lasso, while English saddles have a flat front ("pommel") to make jumping easy. Trick riding saddles

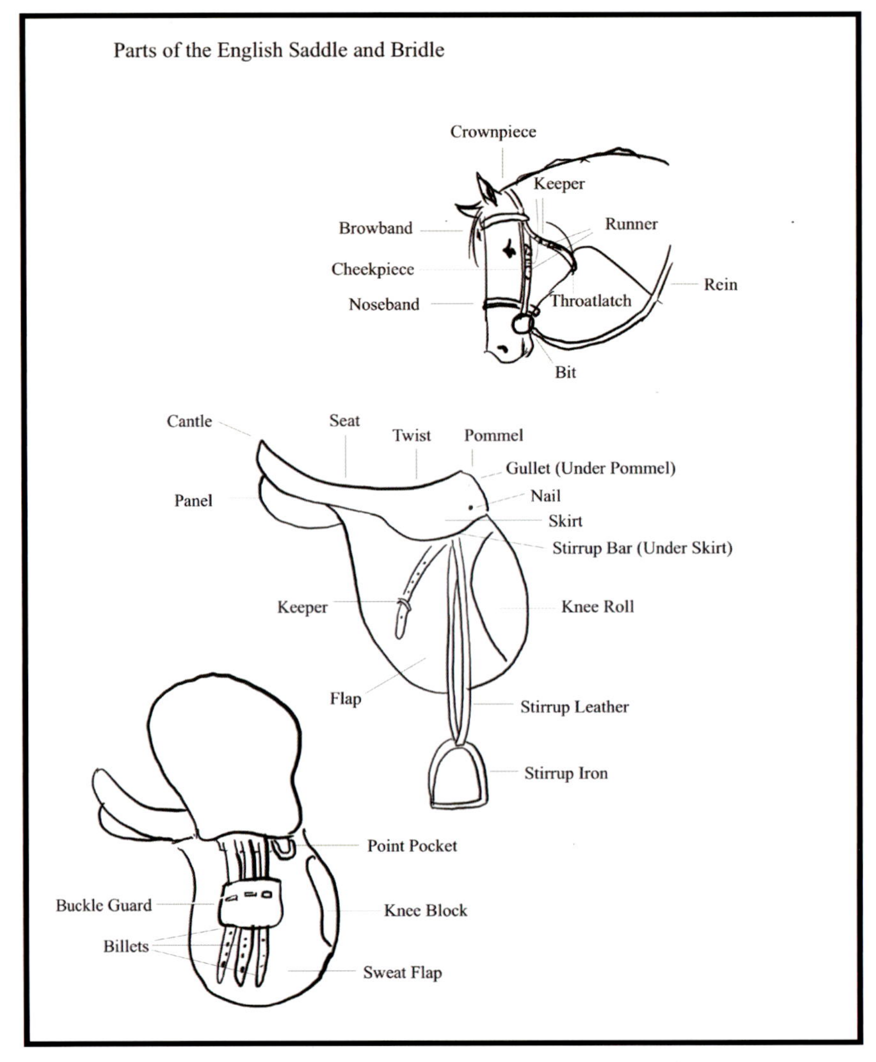

have a long, skinny horn that acts like a handle to help the rider do tricks.

Other riding tack styles include Australian, working equitation, sidesaddle, and endurance racing. Many countries have saddles that perform the same jobs but look unique.

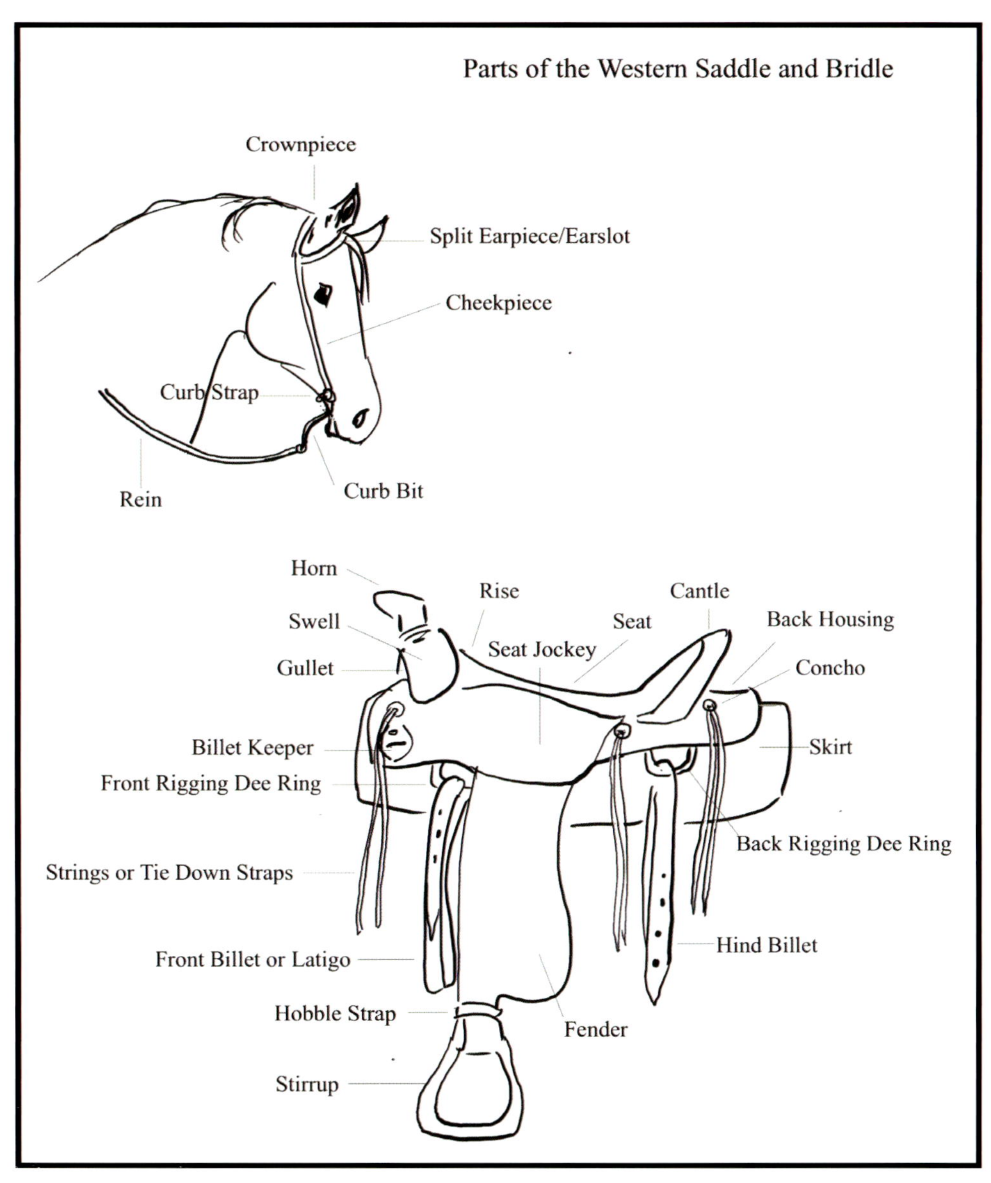

Bridling

1. Unfasten the crownpiece of the halter, slide the noseband just off your horse's nose, and re-buckle or retie the crownpiece behind his ears. This way your horse is still tied and won't wander away. Put the reins over your horse's head.
2. Hold the bridle with the crownpiece in your right hand and the bit flat across your left hand. If your horse is cross-tied, stand behind the cross-ties, next to him. Face forward and bring your right hand up by his poll, between his ears, and towards his forehead. If his head is too high, you can also bring your right arm under his head and grasp the bridle just below the browband.
3. Place the bit at the front of his lips with your fingers flat, so you do not get nipped by accident. Many horses learn to open their mouths for the bit. You may need to slide the thumb of your left hand between the corners of his lips to encourage him. Horses have no teeth in this area, so it is important to do this correctly.
4. When your horse opens his mouth, bring the bridle towards his ears until the bit is secure in his mouth. Carefully draw the crownpiece into place, folding each ear forward from the base with your left hand. Never fold the ear itself! Gently free any mane hair caught under the crownpiece.

5. Buckle the throatlatch, making sure it is not twisted. You should be able to fit four fingers between your horse's throat and the throatlatch—loose enough to let him breathe freely when he flexes, but snug enough to keep the bridle in place in a mishap. Run the end of the strap through the keeper and the runner. If you want a polished turnout, position the runner over the last hole of the throatlatch.

> Many people cut or shave their horse's mane a few inches behind his ears. This "bridle path" gives the crownpiece a comfortable place to sit. Different breeds and disciplines have different customs for bridle paths. Most English sports trim bridle paths just enough to clear the crownpiece, while gaited breeds often shave up to 12 inches. The manes of Polo ponies and Three-gaited Saddlebreds are entirely shaved!

6. Place the noseband straps between the cheekpieces and your horse's face. Make sure the noseband is straight. Fasten the buckle, and tuck the strap through the keeper and runner, just like you did with the throatlatch.
7. Remember how we said we would tighten the girth bit by bit? Gently snug it up a hole or two. Make sure to tighten it evenly on both sides to keep the girth centered.
8. Double check that the bridle looks straight and tidy. Unclip the cross-ties or lead rope from the halter, unfasten the

crownpiece, and hang the halter on the wall. Never leave a halter clipped to the cross-tie or crumpled on the ground. It could get stepped on, or tangled in a horse's legs.

Most English saddles have three billets for two important reasons. The different positioning allows you to change the position of the girth. Most horses use the first and third billet. The unused billet is important in an emergency. If a billet strap breaks, buckle the girth to the unused billet. If you ride in the ring, that's not a big deal. But imagine your billet breaking on a trail ride far from home!

9. Bring the reins back over the horse's head. Hold them together in your right hand four inches or so from the bit. Some horses get claustrophobic if you hold too close to the bit. Hold the bight (ends) of the reins in your left hand. Lead your horse to the mounting block, ready to ride!

Untacking

You will untack your horse exactly the reverse of tacking up.

1. Fasten the halter loosely around his neck behind his ears. Clip on the lead rope or cross-ties. Now he is secure and you can untack without worrying about him wandering away.
2. Unbuckle the throatlatch and the noseband under his chin.

3. Some horses raise their heads during unbridling. If his head is too high, the bit will catch painfully on his teeth. Ask him to lower his head with gentle pressure on his poll. Holding the crownpiece in your right hand, gently slide it over his ears. Allow him to open his mouth to release the bit—never jerk it out of his mouth.
4. Hang up the bridle, out of the way. If a hook isn't handy, center the buckle of the reins over the crownpiece and slide it over your left shoulder—the bridle will hang neatly next to your body, leaving your arm and hand free to work.
5. Unbuckle the girth on both sides. Lay it across the saddle. If you are riding western, unfasten the girth (cinch) on the near (left) side only.
6. Holding both the pad and the saddle at the pommel and cantle, lift and slide it sideways off the horses back. Place it on a saddle rack.

Final Grooming

Pick your horse's hooves to make sure he did not pick up any stones during your ride. Check his legs for scratches or injuries.

Brush your horse with the body brush or soft brush. Remove any marks left by the saddle and bridle. If your horse is sweaty, you can sponge or hose him. If the weather is cold, cover him with a sweat sheet or fleece cooler until he dries.

Tips for Treats

Many horsemen like to give treats to their horses for a reward or just for fun. Treats should be healthy and nutritious. Sliced up apples and carrots are good choices. Never feed them grass clippings from mown lawns! Ask your instructor or vet what treats are safe for horses.

Offer the treat on your palm with your hand flat. Remember, "fingers flat to feed." Otherwise, your horse might bite your finger instead!

If your horse gets pushy or nippy, put the treat in his feed bucket instead. Some owners do not allow treats. Always respect their decision—there is usually a very good reason!

HANDS-ON HORSES

We touch our horses to communicate, to groom, to make them feel good, and to strengthen our bond. We can expand our routine to include other helpful forms of touch.

- **Equine massage** incorporates different bodywork techniques on the horse's muscles and soft tissue to promote relaxation, circulation, healing, and bonding. While professionals undergo thorough training before they can be certified, you can learn basic techniques to practice on your horse.
- **Stretches** are gentle exercises that improve the range of motion in your horse's neck, legs, back, and body. Sometimes treats are used to encourage the horse to bend and stretch.
- **Acupressure** was developed as a traditional medical practice, with a long history, especially in China. Pressure is applied to specific points along a horse's meridians (energy channels) to open flow, decrease pain, and enhance healing. Acupuncture is very similar but uses needles to stimulate the points.
- **T-Touch** is a special system of bodywork created by Linda Tellington-Jones that uses specific patterns and pressures. Often these touches are applied to acupressure points.

7

Before the Barn: The Basics of the Balanced Seat

You know more about the way horses think, how they communicate with each other, and ways we can communicate with them. You have learned to groom and tack up your favorite horse. Now, let's talk about riding!

This chapter is all about how we go from being a human to becoming a *rider*. We will talk about what position is most effective. We will learn how our own anatomy (the makeup of our body parts) works in the saddle.

We will work through exercises and play fun games with horse-crazy friends. They may not look like riding but they will bring you new awareness, understanding, and control of the body you have lived in all your life. We'll also discuss *why* each point is important, and *how* it makes you a better rider.

By the time you get to the barn, you will have a clear picture in your mind and some muscle memory already stored in your body. You will be a better rider right from the start!

The Big Myth

"Riding is easy, you just sit there! The horse does all the work!"

How many times have you heard this? There are several big lies in this. Riding is not easy, and a good rider does a lot of work, all while making it look like she is sitting still. This takes a great deal of strength, coordination, and the sense of awareness we call "feel." The horse's body moves in all different directions. The rider's body needs to be able to follow all of that movement.

Greek mythology tells tales of centaurs, creatures with the body and legs of a horse and the head, torso, and arms of a human. Nowadays, "centaur" is a high compliment and goal for a rider. We say a team is like a centaur when the horse and rider are so at ease and in tune with each other they seem to be one being.

Our position on the horse is called the "seat," even though our actual seat is just part of it! Our goal is to develop what we call an "independent seat," where we have supple, refined control of our hands, legs, back, and yes, our actual seat itself. Often a beginning rider will find that when she tries to use an aid, other body parts automatically react, giving the horse mixed commands. A rider with an independent seat is able to use each aid separately from the others, or in perfect harmony.

Learning to ride happens in two stages. First, we need to learn how to balance ourselves without gripping or hanging onto the reins for balance. This would interfere with the horse's movement, or worse, cause discomfort or pain. Then we learn how to deliberately "interfere" in a positive way to influence the horse's movement and behavior with our gentle, correct aids.

You can start developing an independent seat before you even get to the barn. Exercises and games you learn on the ground can develop muscle memory. When you get in the saddle, you will become a better rider faster.

The "Balanced Seat"

Look at photos of great riders across different sports and disciplines. If you let your imagination take away the tack, you can see the riders' positions are very similar. All riding styles are founded on what we call the "balanced seat." This means that we keep our center of gravity balanced over our horse's center of gravity, and over our own feet.

What is a "center of gravity?" It is your exact middle, your point of perfect balance. As long as you balance your center of gravity over your feet you can stand, run, leap, dance, *ride*! A rider's center of gravity is deep in her lower belly. Let's find it now!

Sit or stand comfortably but straight. Put your thumb in your belly button and lower your fingers over your tummy. Place the other hand flat across your back at approximately the same height. Your center of gravity lies between your two hands.

The horse's center of gravity is a little bit behind her elbow. A well-fitting saddle will place the rider's weight directly over this spot, where the horse will be able to easily carry the

Martial arts are great cross-training for horsemanship. In fact, a wide-legged, bent-knee position is called the "horse stance." Martial arts teach physical and mental skills that can also help you in the saddle. While many forms stress fighting, others, such as Tai Chi, Aikido, and Chi Gong, are more peaceful. See if you can take a few classes! Make sure to tell the instructor what you know about your center, and how you want to learn to ride better.

Other great sports to help your horsemanship are dancing, fencing, and anything that teaches balance, strength, and flexibility.

weight, and the rider can easily balance. If the rider is behind or ahead of the horse's center of gravity, both beings will struggle.

But what about riders who do not have that straight "plumb line?" Jumpers are a perfect example. You will find that the rider's center of gravity is still stacked over his feet, and over the horse's center of gravity. If the seat comes behind the line, the upper body is usually the same amount in front of the line.

Imagine a line dropping straight down from a rider's ear. Does it go through his shoulder, hip, and heel on the way to the ground? You can also imagine the rider's "sections" as a tower of blocks: your head, your shoulders, your middle, your seat, and your legs/feet. The blocks should stack evenly to build a strong structure that won't topple over.

The Power of the Pelvis

Did you know you have a bucket at the bottom of your belly? Your pelvis is a group of bones at the base of your body. When you are born, the bones are separate. As you get older, the bones fuse together almost in the shape of a grain bucket!

Why are we talking about your pelvis? Your pelvis contains your center of gravity and energy. It connects your upper body to your legs and these body parts are vital for good riding. Many times a single correction to your pelvis will cause a chain reaction through your back to your head and down to your toes, improving your entire position.

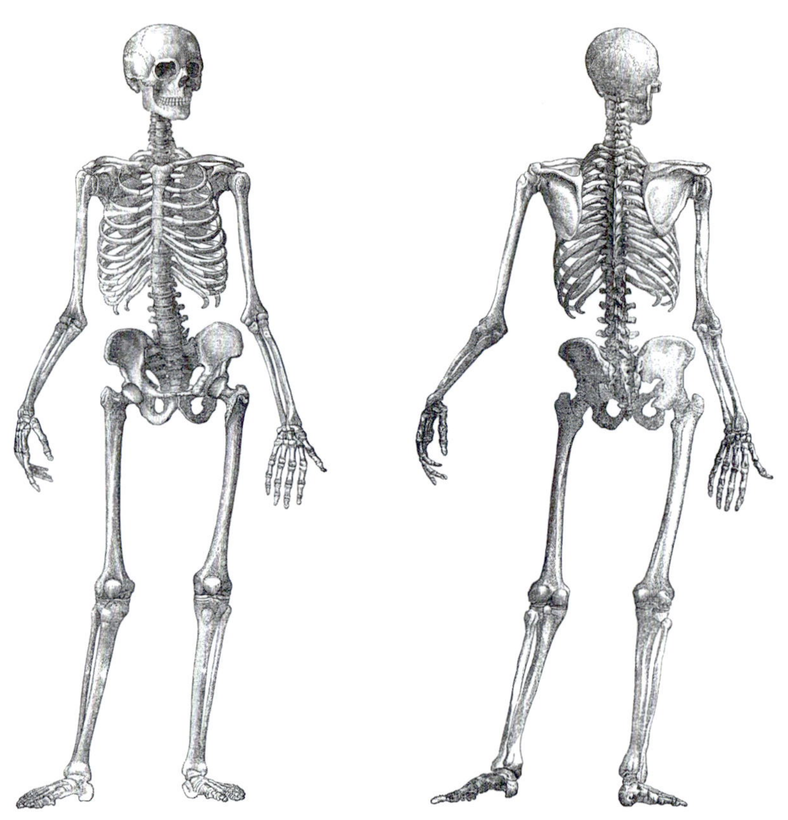

Put your hand back on your center, thumb in belly button, palm on your lower tummy. Now move your hand side to side without raising or lowering it. Feel those bony lumps? Those are your hip bones, the top of your pelvis.

Now sit on your hands, palms up. Feel those bony lumps? Those are your seat bones. Slowly move your upper body forward, then waaaay back. Feel how the pressure on your seat bones changed? When your body is balanced upright over your center of gravity, your pelvis is balanced, and your seat bones are pointing directly below you. Memorize this feeling: this is the foundation of a beautifully balanced seat in the saddle!

What a Feat!

Take a minute to think about your feet. Take off your shoes and socks and wiggle your toes. Lift your heels and then your toes. Look all the different ways your amazing feet can move!

When we stand or skip or run, our feet act as middlemen between our moving body and the earth. They have the same job in the saddle—but instead of solid ground, they need to balance on the stirrup.

Do you have a horse-crazy friend? Do these unmounted exercises together! Take turns watching each other. You will notice new things in each other. You will combine the power of all of your senses to see into each other's "blind spots," habits and postures that are so much a part of you that you are not even aware of them. Plus, everything is more fun with a friend!

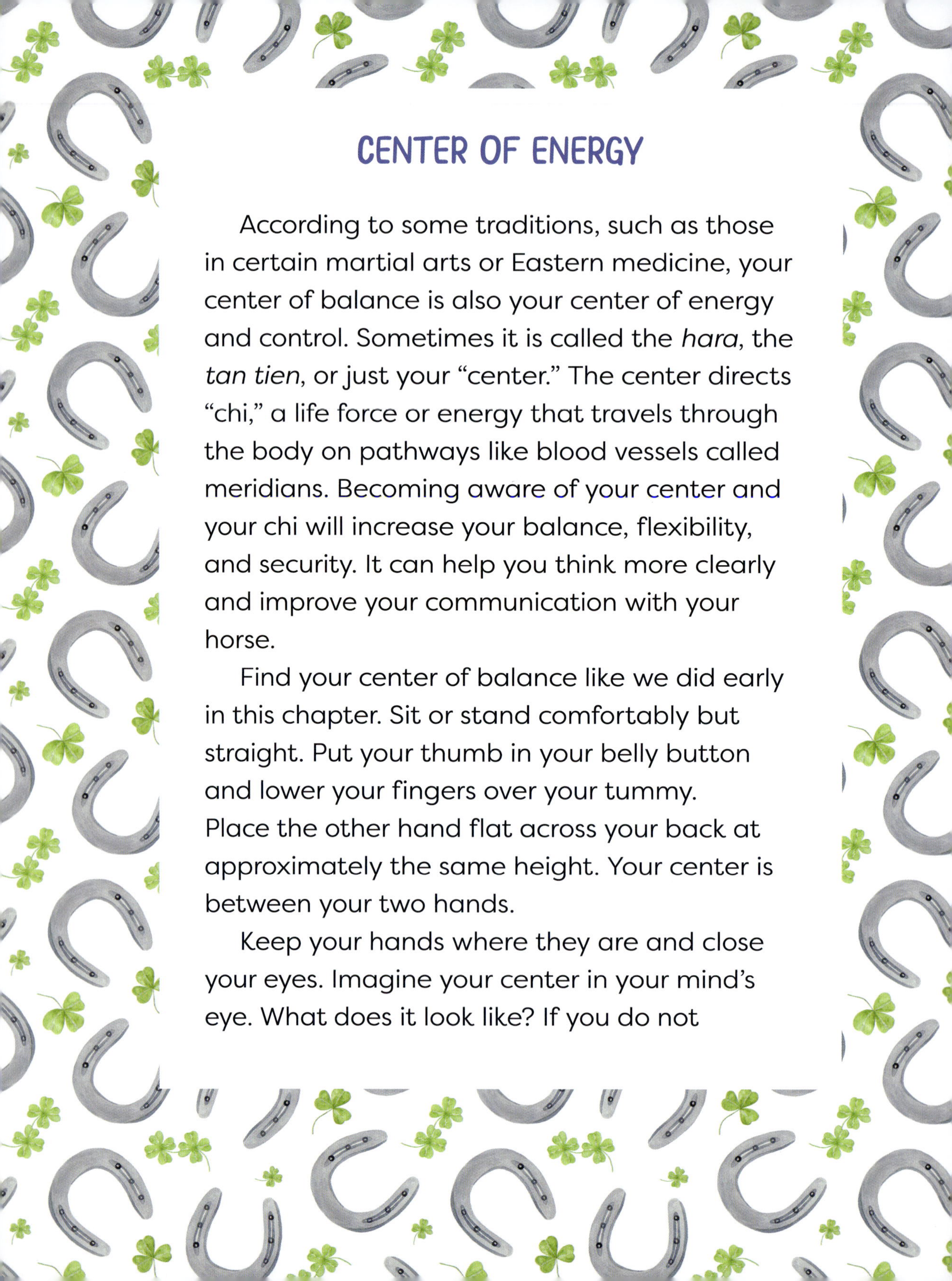

CENTER OF ENERGY

According to some traditions, such as those in certain martial arts or Eastern medicine, your center of balance is also your center of energy and control. Sometimes it is called the *hara*, the *tan tien*, or just your "center." The center directs "chi," a life force or energy that travels through the body on pathways like blood vessels called meridians. Becoming aware of your center and your chi will increase your balance, flexibility, and security. It can help you think more clearly and improve your communication with your horse.

Find your center of balance like we did early in this chapter. Sit or stand comfortably but straight. Put your thumb in your belly button and lower your fingers over your tummy. Place the other hand flat across your back at approximately the same height. Your center is between your two hands.

Keep your hands where they are and close your eyes. Imagine your center in your mind's eye. What does it look like? If you do not imagine anything, do not worry, you can help it along! Picture it as a ball. What color is it? Does it have a sound? Does it have movement? There are no right or wrong answers, only *your* answers!

Pay attention to your breath. How far down does your breath go? Does it feel like it stops in your throat? Does it feel like it gets as far as your lungs? Imagine your body is an empty tube. Can you draw your breath as far down as your feet? Maybe your center is breathing along with your lungs, expanding and relaxing as you inhale and exhale.

Check in with the rest of your body. Has anything changed since you were focusing on your center? Most times you will find your muscles have relaxed, your breathing has deepened, your awareness has increased, and your balance has improved. Can you see how this could be a powerful tool in the saddle? How do you think your horse will respond to these changes? Now try it during your next ride!

Look at the soles (bottoms) of your feet. The wide, padded parts of your foot where the toes connect are called the balls of your feet. Placing your stirrups directly under the balls of your feet will offer solidity and flexibility: the perfect foundation for your balanced seat!

Find a step with a solid railing. Stand on the lowest step with your hand on the railing. Place the balls of your feet securely on the edge of the step. Relax your ankles. Feel how your heels sink down? This is what will happen when your feet are in the stirrups.

Gently explore different movements. Stand on tiptoe. Do you feel how wobbly you become? This is what will happen if you brace against your stirrups while you ride. Relax your ankle and sink into your heels again. Ahhhhh!

Try widening the distance between your feet and bending your knees as if you were on a horse. How does this change your balance and security? Take a break if your feet or legs need a rest. This is hard work!

Keep a hold on the railing and stay on the bottom step for this—it is not as easy as it looks!

Now, stand in the same position on the step, holding the rail, balanced on the balls of your feet. Stretch up through the top of your head. It should feel like you're growing taller. Keep this growing taller feeling, and

> You have 26 bones and over a hundred muscles, ligaments, and tendons in each foot. That's a lot to lace into each boot!

slooowly push your pelvis/seat behind you. Keep your center of gravity over your feet.

Allow your body to lean forward but stay strong through your middle. Remember, you are still growing out the top of your head, but now you're growing forward as well as upward. Come back to upright position and take a rest.

What you just felt was a perfect jumping position: strong, elegant, and beautifully balanced over your feet. What are some other things that feel similar, even if they have nothing to do with horses? Some real world examples are playing leapfrog, jumping down off a ledge, or downhill skiing (especially over moguls!).

Mirror, Mirror on the Wall

What you do when you're not thinking will become your habit. More often than not, the posture you have just hanging around will be the posture that you have in the saddle. Our goal is to change those habits that keep you from becoming the best rider you can be. But you cannot make these changes unless you can feel what needs to be changed, and to each of us, our habits feel "normal."

We are in our best balance when the two sides of our body are close to "symmetrical," that is, mirror images. Just the fact that we are right- or left-handed means that symmetry is disturbed. But if we are aware of it, we can improve it!

You can play this game with a friend, or in front of a mirror if you are by yourself. Close your eyes. Stand "normally."

Ask your friend to describe what she sees. We'll call this a position scan. Here are some questions she can ask (or you can ask yourself): Seen from the side, is there a straight line dropped down from your ear, through your shoulders, hips and heels? Are your shoulders open, or rounded? Is one shoulder in front of the other or are they even?

Have her look at you from the front or back. Is your head level? Is one shoulder scrunched higher than the other? What about your hips? Are they level and even? Are your feet the same distance from your body? Do your toes point out the same amount? Usually what feels "normal" is far from straight and symmetrical!

Now close your eyes again. Think about what you just learned about your "normal." Stand as straight and symmetrical as possible with your eyes closed. Have your friend scan your position again, asking the same questions.

What did you discover?

This exercise reveals that our impressions of ourselves are often askew. But it is the first step in developing awareness and accurate feel. Now you know that when you feel straight, your shoulders are actually rounded, for example. You can remind yourself to stretch tall and open your shoulders as you go through your day. The more you practice on the ground, the more good habits will replace old habits, and the faster your riding will improve.

Play Horse

You have probably already played this next game hundreds of times! Go outside. Pretend you're a horse. Stamp, snort, whinny! Act like a wild mustang—or your favorite frisky horse on the first chilly winter morning. Have you got out all your bucks and kicks? Good, time to settle down to work.

Begin walking. Not a mosey, but the rhythmic, energetic walk you want on a fun trail ride or strutting your stuff in the show ring. Send your awareness into your pelvis. Remember we said it is the foundation of a balanced, effective seat.

> **Bonus Tip:** If the footing is safe, shut your eyes and let your friends lead you by the hand. Closing your eyes often helps allow you to feel more clearly.

Feel how softly your hips swing in so many directions. Side to side, up and down, forward and backward. This is the same movement your seat will make when it is following the movement of the horses back.

Now pick up a trot (or jog). What changes? What is similar? Feel how much more jolting it is? No wonder it can be so hard to ride! Do not worry—soon you will be able to follow the movements like a pro!

Now canter. (If you haven't played horse before, cantering is like skipping without hopping twice on the same leg.) Unlike the walk and trot, the foot falls have an uneven rhythm. That moment when all your legs are off the ground—or when your horse's legs are off the ground—is called the "moment of suspension."

Feel how your hips move forward a little bit following your legs and how one leg moves more forward than the other? The movement your hips make is the same as when riding. The leg that comes further forward is called the leading leg. When the horse canters, it will be easiest to balance if he leads with the inside leg. Is it easier for you, too?

Why do you think we played this game, especially if you have played horse a million times? There are lot of different answers. You will find one explanation in the next chapter. Until then, think about it, experiment playing horse, and write your discoveries in your journal!

Now you have a clear picture in your mind's eye of what of what a balanced seat looks like. You are practicing tuning in to your body. You are discovering new ways to move your body that will help to give accurate aids or signals to the horse. Let's go to the barn and tack up!

8

Riding Lessons: In the Saddle

In the last chapter, you learned about effective position in the saddle. You started developing the body awareness of a rider by moving like a horse on your own two feet. You have learned to safely catch, groom, and tack up your horse. Now, let's ride!

What to Wear?

Some instructors will ask you to dress a certain way. Even if they do not have a dress code, you will want to be comfortable. Most of all, you want to be safe and athletic. Follow these simple suggestions to help you ride your best.

What	Why
A well-fitting ASTM/SEI-approved riding helmet every single ride	To protect your precious brain!
A safety vest	To protect your spine and organs in case of a fall
Riding boots (short or tall) with a smooth sole and distinct heel	To prevent getting trapped in the stirrup
Long pants that are comfortable and don't limit your flexibility	To avoid rubs and allow you to ride your best
Close-fitting shirt or sweater	To allow your instructor to see your position, and to prevent getting snagged on your saddle
Riding gloves	To grip sweaty, slippery reins, or to keep warm in winter
No loose jewelry or scarves	To avoid getting tangled in your tack or choking
No candy or gum	To prevent accidentally choking

At the Mounting Block

1. Line your horse up so your saddle is even with the mounting block. If you are riding English, pull the stirrups down.
2. Check your girth or cinch and tighten again if needed. The girth should be just tight enough to slide your hand between the skin and the girth, but you should not be able to pull the girth away from your horse's side.
3. Step to the top of the block. With your left hand, hold both reins and a handful of the horse's mane close to the pommel. If you hold the pommel or horn itself, the saddle could twist painfully on your horse's back.

4. Twist your stirrup counterclockwise. Slide your left foot into the stirrup, making sure not to dig the horse with your toe. Push off of your right leg, taking your weight in your left foot in the stirrup. Swing your right leg up over the cantle, making sure not to brush your horse's back with your foot. Gently lower yourself into the saddle.
5. Put your right foot in the stirrup. At first you may need to use your hand to line the stirrup up with your foot. Make sure to twist it clockwise so the stirrup leather lies comfortably against your leg. If it's twisted, you may get a nasty rub!
6. Take your right rein with your right hand. Straighten out any twists in the reins and adjust them to even lengths.

Congratulations! You are now in sitting in the best place in the world: on the back of a horse!

Settled in the Saddle

Take a minute to settle in. Can you feel your horse's back through the saddle? Can you feel him breathing? Can you match your breath with his?

Think back to "The Power of the Pelvis" section in chapter 7. You may want to read it again, and do the exercise, just before you go to the barn. Now do the same exercise on horseback.

Balance on your seat bones. Slowly lean too far forward, keeping your legs directly beneath you, next to the girth. Where does that put pressure? Now lean too far back. Do you feel how are the pressure changes in your seat bones? Slowly rock forward and back until you feel like you're sitting up straight with your seat bones pointing directly down underneath you. That's a good balanced foundation!

Walk On!

With your legs hanging directly underneath your hips, lightly squeeze both calves to ask your horse to walk. If you listen to the footfalls, you will hear that the walk has four beats. Watch how the head and neck move. Your hands will need to move forwards and back to follow that motion. We call this a "following hand."

Feel the movement of your horse's back and allow it to gently shift your seat and body. We call this a "following seat."

Time to Turn

Your horse feels small shifts in your weight. Turn your head in the direction you want to go. Allow your body to turn as well. Imagine shining a flashlight from your belly button in the same direction you are looking. This will change your weight in the saddle. Move your inside hand slightly away from your horse's neck to "lead" him through the turn. Allow him to bend by "following" with your outside hand.

ADJUSTING YOUR GIRTH AND STIRRUPS FROM THE SADDLE

Often, a girth will need to be tightened once your weight is in the saddle, or once the horse has warmed up a little bit. At first, your instructor will help you. Once you are secure in the saddle, you will learn to do this by yourself.

1. Hold both reins in one hand.
2. Keeping your foot in the stirrup, lift your leg or bring it completely in front of the saddle flap. Grasp the billet or latigo close to the buckle and gently pull up to tighten the girth.
3. While still holding the billet, use your pointer finger to put the buckle toggle into the hole.
4. Repeat with the other billet. If you are riding Western and use a latigo knot, you will probably need to dismount to adjust the cinch.

Your stirrups are easier to adjust.

1. Lift your foot slightly to take the weight off while keeping it in the stirrup.
2. Lift your knee enough to grasp the buckle.
3. If you are riding western, you may need to slide a metal plate away from the buckle.
4. Use your pointer finger to move the tongue of the buckle out of and into the holes.
5. Adjust the stirrup to the length you want, and pull the bottom of the leather to slide the buckle back up to the stirrup bar.

Test Your Brakes

Stretch up tall and squeeze your shoulders back. This engages your core muscles, that is, the muscles in your stomach and back. This is such a powerful aid that sometimes it is enough!

Exhale or say "whoa." English riders sometimes say "ho." Stop your arms from following the movement of the horse's head and neck while squeezing both fists evenly on the reins. As soon as the horse stops, soften your fists and praise your horse for a halt well done.

"ON THE GIRTH"

The basic leg placement is what we call "on the girth." The rider's leg hangs freely. Her heel is beneath her hip. The stirrup leather appears vertical with the ground, close to the girth. This position gives the rider the greatest balance, security, and control.

The rider may slide her leg back a few inches into a position called "behind the girth." In this position, the leg is giving the horse specific cues. It is asking the horse to shift his hind quarters away from the leg pressure, or to transition to canter. Once the aid is given, the rider's leg returns to its placement on the girth.

Trot On

Squeeze both legs on the girth to ask the horse to trot. It is going to feel bouncy at first! Hold a piece of mane, a neck strap, or your saddle's pommel or horn until you get the hang of it.

Sitting trot requires your seat to follow the bouncing of your horse's back. This demands core (stomach and back) strength and flexibility. Think of letting your seat bones drop down alternately to follow the movement of your horse's back. Reread the last chapter and practice playing horse. Feel how, when you are trotting on foot, those seat bones alternately drop and rise? Now find that feeling in the saddle.

The horse's head and neck do not move forward and back in the trot the way they do in the walk. Your hands and arms must remain quietly independent of the motion of the rest of your body to prevent pulling on the reins.

Posting Trot

Riders learned hundreds of years ago it was easier for both horse and rider to "post," that is, to stand and sit with the horse's natural trot rhythm. Let the horse's thrust lift you out of the saddle for a beat, then sit on the next beat. Sometimes it helps to sing a song in rhythm with the trot, or chant "up-down-up-down."

> An easy way to remember the correct diagonal is to think, "rise and fall with the leg to the wall." Memorize this rhyme and you will always be right!

Posting can be difficult if you are leaning too far forward or trying to pull yourself up with your shoulders. Instead, imagine a bungee cord connects your belt buckle to your horse's ears. After each time you sit, the bungee cord springs your hips forward and up.

Once you master the act of posting, you will learn your diagonals. When a horse trots, she moves her legs in diagonal pairs. When the left hind and right front move forward together we call it the right diagonal. When the right hind and left front move together, we call it the left diagonal.

Riders usually post on the outside diagonal. This means you will stand when it looks like the horse's outside shoulder is swinging forward and sit when it is swinging back.

The Enchanting Canter

Now ask your horse to canter. At first, your instructor will cue the horse for you. Different horses may be trained with different cues. Most will canter with a light squeeze of the rider's outside leg behind the girth, and a cluck, kiss, or spoken "can-TER."

ONE POSITION, THREE NAMES

Jump position, half seat, and two-point position all mean the same thing. The rider's seat is held just above the saddle, slightly further back than usual. Her center of gravity is balanced over her legs. Her body leans forward while lifting tall and straight. The bouncing of the gaits or jump is absorbed by her flexing knees and ankles. All of her weight is carried by her legs and feet.

The half seat lets the horse work or go longer distances without getting tired, as the rider's weight is not on his back. It allows the rider to stay in balance, while galloping at speed or jumping over obstacles. It is also a great tool to build strength, endurance, and a sense of rhythm.

Even if you have no plans to learn how to jump, practicing your half seat will improve your riding. Shorten your stirrups a few holes. Hold your horse's mane or a neck strap (a strap such as a stirrup leather buckled around the horse's neck) for balance so you don't risk pulling the reins. Practice the halt and walk before you work your way up to trot and canter. Gradually hold your half seat for longer distances to build your strength.

The first thing you'll notice is that unlike the walk and trot, the foot falls have an uneven rhythm. That moment when all four feet are off the ground is called the moment of suspension. Sit deep in the saddle without leaning forward, gripping with your legs, or bracing against your stirrups. Hold on to your horn or pommel to help keep a deep seat. Let your seat follow the rocking-horse movement.

The horse's head and neck will move even more in the canter than it did in the walk. Allow your hands and arms to freely follow that motion without pulling the reins. It helps to learn to canter on the lunge line, so you can focus on learning to ride the gait without worrying about control.

The sequence of footfalls in the canter end with the horse reaching further forward with one foreleg than the other. We call these "leads." The horse is most balanced when she is on the inside lead, that is, reaching further forward with her inside front leg. Cantering on the outside lead is called "counter canter." "Cross cantering" occurs when the horse's front legs are on one lead and her hind legs are on the other. With practice, you will learn to feel these different leads.

Dismounting

After your ride, halt your horse in a safe, flat area.

1. Take both feet out of the stirrups.
2. Place your reins (and your crop if used) in your left hand, then put your left hand on your horse's neck or withers. Put your right hand on the withers or pommel/horn.
3. Lean forward while swinging your right leg high over the cantle. Take care not to kick your horse's back or rump!
4. Twist your body as you slide down, so you land facing forward. Bend your knees slightly to land gently.
5. Take the reins over your horse's neck. Slide the stirrups up to the bars and tuck the leathers between the stirrup and the saddle flap. Loosen the girth or cinch a hole or two.

For the first several rides, your instructor may have your horse on the lead line or a lunge line. This will let you focus on learning all you can through your senses without having to worry about controlling the horse at the same time. You may also do gymnastic exercises to help develop your independent seat. At the historic Spanish Riding School in Vienna, Austria, new riders remain on the lunge line for up to two years!

A SEAT FOR EACH SEASON

There is a seat for each season, when you ride for a reason!

The western seat, or stock seat, started with the Spanish conquistadores and evolved from the ranching traditions of the American West. The saddle is large and heavy, with a high cantle and a horn used to dally (secure) lariats for working cattle. It is designed to be comfortable for both horse and rider on a long day of work.

The western rider sits with a balanced seat and a long leg. She holds the reins in one hand, leaving the other hand free for working and roping. Most western horses are trained to neck rein; that is, to turn off the pressure of the rein against the neck rather than the bit in the mouth. They are typically ridden in a curb bit on a loose rein.

English riding includes several variations. Specialty saddles support the different goals of the various seats. The hunt seat began with Europeans who would ride at high speeds across the rugged countryside, jumping whatever

obstacles were in their path. It is now seen in the show ring in the Hunter and Jumper divisions. It is characterized by a light, forward position.

The dressage seat is deep, flexible, and upright. It looks similar to the western seat because they share roots in the Iberian training traditions of Spain and Portugal. Unlike western riders, dressage riders maintain contact with their horses' mouths through the reins.

Saddle seat arose from long hours in the saddle when horses were used as transport. Some saddle seat horses, such as Tennessee Walkers, are gaited. This means they have special paces beyond the walk, trot, and canter that are extra smooth and extremely comfortable to ride. Most saddle seat horses are bred to look flashy, like a fancy car, with a high head carriage and leg action. Saddle seat riders sit further back on their horses, with higher hands and a more forward leg position.

Other riding styles you might see include racing, polo, sidesaddle, endurance riding, and bareback.

9

Show Off!

As you progress in your reading and your riding, you will discover that there are almost as many ways to enjoy horses as there are horses to enjoy them with. Some activities are competitive. Some are just plain fun!

Horses have worked hard with their humans throughout history. But when the work is done, it is time to play! Most games and horse show classes developed out of different working traditions around the globe.

Horse Shows at a Glance

Most horse shows offer different "divisions," which include several classes (usually between three and five). Divisions may be determined by the age or experience level of the rider or horse, number of classes won in the past, height of fences in a jumping course, and so on.

Scores from the classes are added up to determine the division's champion and reserve champion (the second-highest placed horse/rider team). The show may offer a high point rider or horse award at the end of the day. A show series or association may also offer year-end championship awards.

Pleasure classes are judged on the horse's attitude and way of going. He should look like a pleasure to ride! His rider looks as if she is doing nothing because the horse is so tuned to her aids. Equitation classes are judged on the rider's position and effectiveness. Working classes judge the horse's ability for the job at hand, such as working hunter or working cow horse. Trail classes include obstacles that mimic challenges you might come across on a trail ride. Lead line classes are for the youngest rider, whose pony is led by a parent or a friend.

Riders and horses are judged against the standard for their discipline. The outlines, attitudes, and energy levels of western pleasure winners will look completely different than those of park pleasure champions. Often a horse and rider who are frustrated or unsuccessful in one discipline will shine when shown in more suitable classes.

A Closer Look at English Shows

English shows offer a variety of divisions. Hunters are judged on their style and manners on the flat and over fences. Show jumpers clear huge fences at a fast gallop. Dressage horses are scored on their obedience and movement through intricate patterns, like ballet.

Three-phase eventing, also called three-day eventing or combined training, tests a horse's training, versatility, and endurance. Horses must complete tests in dressage, show jumping, and cross-country jumping over varied terrain.

Sidesaddle classes showcase ladies in long dresses riding in historical sidesaddles. The horns of a sidesaddle offer the rider great security while both legs are positioned on the same side of the horse.

Saddle seat, also called park classes, highlight the style of riding that shows off high-stepping horses, most notably Saddlebreds.

Fox chasers follow a pack of hounds following the scent of a fox. A drag hunt follows a scented trail laid ahead of time by volunteer riders. Fox chasing offers several competitive opportunities. In a mock hunt, riders dressed up as the foxes lay a trail, often of popcorn, while other riders play the parts of the hounds, and the various members of the riding staff. A hunter pace consists of a course laid out across country. Riders compete in teams of two or more. The winners are the ones who come closest to the ideal time a typical fox chaser would take over the same course.

Working equitation is an obstacle course ridden at speed based on an Iberian (Spanish or Portuguese) ranch horse's daily work. While it is performed in an Iberian or English saddle, it looks like a combination of dressage and trail class. Western riding developed from the horsemanship heritage of the Spanish conquistadores, and working equitation gives us a glimpse into those traditions.

A Closer Look at Western Shows

Western shows also host a wide selection of classes in addition to pleasure, equitation (also called horsemanship), working, trail, and lead line.

Cattle cutting judges the horse's ability to separate a specific cow from the herd. The best "cow horses" do their job on their own, without cues from the rider. **Team penning** involves three riders who work together to cut three particular cows from the herd and drive them into a pen at the opposite end of the arena.

Reining involves riding a pattern that includes spins, high speed circles, and sliding stops. **Western dressage** combines western riding with traditional dressage.

Rodeos include speed events based on ranch work. **Bareback riding** and **saddle bronc riding** challenge riders to stay on bucking horses for at least eight seconds. **Calf roping** demands a

galloping rider rope a calf, dismount, and tie three of the calf's legs together. **Team roping** requires a team of two riders to lasso the horns and hind legs of a cow. **Barrel racing** involves galloping a cloverleaf pattern around barrels set up in a large triangle.

Drive On!

Carriage driving celebrates when horses were used for human transportation. **Fine harness** classes highlight high-stepping horses such as Saddlebreds and Hackneys. **Roadster** classes celebrate speed and well as style.

Combined driving, similar to three-day eventing, tests a horse in driven dressage as well as obstacle courses across country ("marathon") and in the arena ("cones"). **Pleasure driving** judges a horse's manners and obedience.

Pulling contests challenge horses to pull the heaviest weights. Driving horses range from tiny miniature horses to massive draft breeds. Horses can pull a vehicle alone, or with one or more other horses as part of a "team" or a "hitch."

A Breed Apart

Many breed registries sponsor regional, national, and even world championships. They can encompass English, western, dressage, and even carriage driving. Breed shows often reward versatility, which is the ability for one horse to perform in multiple disciplines.

Some breed registries reward successes won through open (nonbreed) shows. Winners receive additional prizes and awards.

REAL HORSES, REAL RIDERS

As a teen, Mary was drawn to Morgans. Mary and her Morgan gelding, Puff, won countless national and world championships in many different disciplines, even carriage driving!

"Thanks to Puff and his talents, it made me a more rounded horse person because I was able to try out different divisions," said Mary. "I ended up doing all the different things with him because *he* was good at them! It was kind of like being an intern at a big company and getting to try out different things before deciding what to focus on for a career."

The Need for Speed

Every equestrian culture features horse racing in many forms.

Thoroughbred racing, or flat racing, is also called the sport of kings. Races take place on oval tracks which may be dirt, turf, or synthetic footing. In any country, races are run in one direction only. For example, in the United States they are always run counterclockwise while in England they are always run clockwise.

Historical races could be many miles long or run in heats (several races in a row, separated by a brief rest period). Perhaps the most famous horse race in the United States is the Kentucky Derby, also known as the Run for the Roses for the garland of red roses draped over the winner's neck.

> Racing is probably the oldest horse sport. The Olympic Games included racing as early as 648 BCE!

The Kentucky Derby, along with the Preakness Stakes and the Belmont Stakes, make up the famous "Triple Crown." As of 2025, only 13 thoroughbreds had won all three races to become celebrated Triple Crown champions.

While Thoroughbred racing is the most common, other breeds are raced as well. In the United States, there are races for Quarter Horses, Appaloosas, Arabians, and Paints. Some rodeos and foxhunts offer races for any breed of horse. There are even races just for ponies! Indian relay races require riders to change horses several times throughout the race.

Steeplechasing takes the thrill of flat racing and adds jumps. Some steeplechases are run at race tracks over brush jumps. Others are held across open countryside over a variety of different jumps. Steeplechases are also called point-to-points.

In eighteenth-century Ireland, riders would race from one town to another using church steeples, the tallest points in town, as start and finish markers. The name stuck!

Not all races are ridden. **Harness racing** is very popular in the United States and other countries. Horses pull a lightweight cart called a sulky. Horses speed around the track at a trot. Some horses pace, a gait when both legs on the same side on the same side move forward and back together. The most famous harness race in the United States is the Hambletonian.

Not all harness racing takes place at a track. Rodeos and western festivals may host chariot and chuckwagon races.

Drill to Thrill

Mounted **drill rides** consist of intricate patterns ridden to music. Teams can include anywhere from two riders to as many as the arena can hold! The patterns include movements in which the riders appear to weave through, around, and between each other like a dance. Riders need to have a great skill and timing to avoid running into each other!

The Canadian Mounted Police have a world-famous drill team. Their programs include 32 riders mounted on solid black, highly trained horses.

Game On!

The only thing more fun than games are games on horseback! **Mounted games** go by several different names, such as Gymkhana and Play Day. Riders may compete in any style saddle. Competitions may be open either to individuals or relay-race style teams. Popular games include barrel racing, pole bending, sword races, and more.

Some mounted team sports are centered around a ball. **Polo** can be compared to high-speed hockey on horseback. **Polocrosse** is similar to lacrosse played on horseback. **Horseball** uses a large ball suspended in a leather harness with six handles, often requiring players to drop their reins entirely!

Extreme Equestrians

If you are a daredevil, you will love the extreme equine sports! **Skijoring** (skee-YOR-ing) challenges a skier to maneuver around gates and over jumps while being pulled by a galloping horse. **Horseboarding** is similar, but the participant is on a modified skateboard instead of skis. Horseboarders can also be pulled along the edge of a lake or the sea on wake boards.

Vaulting is an elegant sport highlighting one or more gymnasts performing intricate moves on a circling horse. **Trick riders** carry out daring acrobatics, including leaping on and off at high speeds. **Roman riding** challenges riders to stand with their feet on the backs of two horses while performing patterns, including jumps.

While polo vies with racing for the title of "king of horse sports," polocrosse stands alone as "king of the one-horse sports." First played in Australia, polocrosse combines the best of—you guessed it!—polo and lacrosse. While polo players are allowed to change mounts as often as they like through a game, ensuring they are always on a fresh, energetic horse, polocrosse allows each rider only one horse. Riders alternate "chukkas" (periods) to give their horses time to rest between efforts. Polocrosse is not only a test of skill but of the horsemanship required to condition and train an equine partner to play their best throughout the entire match.

Happy Trails

Trail riding sports allow you to enjoy beautiful natural locations. **Endurance races** range from twenty-five miles to a hundred miles or more. **Competitive trail rides** judge a horse's performance as well as speed and fitness.

Competitors in the Mongolian Derby race over six hundred miles of wilderness riding semi-feral Mongolian horses, changing to a fresh horse every 25–30 miles (40–48 km). The Gaucho Derby is a similar race held in Argentina on hardy Criollo horses. Both derbies highlight the deeply rooted horsemanship traditions of the cultures.

Do you like to run? **Ride and tie** events include teams made up of two riders and one horse. Competitors alternate riding with running on foot. The first competitor rides to a designated area, safety ties the horse, and continues on foot. By the time the runner reaches the area, the horse has had a nice rest and a snack and is ready to be ridden to the next station. They will pass the runner along the way, and the horse will again get a rest while the runner catches up. The first team across the finish line is the winner.

Not all trail adventures are competitions. Horseback **trekking** consists of rides through beautiful natural areas. They are often organized around a theme, such as beach rides or exploring castles. Treks can last anywhere from several hours to several weeks!

In-Hand

Not all horse show classes involve a rider or a driver. Many equestrians love competing in in-hand classes, where horses are led rather than ridden or driven.

> You do not need to ride to enjoy horse activities! Write down what you learn about new horse sports in your horse journal. Focus on the ones that look fun or different. Write an article as if you were a journalist reporting on an event. Or write a story where the hero or heroine competes in these competitions. Create drawings to illustrate your writing.

Halter classes evaluate a horse's conformation and temperament against the breed standard for the perfect horse. **Showmanship** classes test the handler's ability to control their horse through specific patterns. **Mini jumping** consists of miniature horses being led over courses of jumps at a trot or canter. **Mule jumping** highlights mules jumping tall fences from a standstill.

Horseless Horse Shows

Some horse shows do not even require a horse! **Model horse shows** are extremely popular. Participants can enter not only their favorite models, but also create tack, equipment, and entire scenes in miniature. Artists may customize models with paint and real hair. They may even use heat guns to soften and reshape the entire model!

Stick horse shows , also called hobby horse shows, are also popular. Competitors "ride" stick horses through patterns and over jumping courses. If you have a lot of energy, this is the perfect division for you!

Time Travel

While many activities reflect history, some go all the way! **Mounted reenacting** explores different time periods of horsemanship. Participants will dress in clothes from the period. Horses will often wear historically accurate tack and costumes. **Medieval reenacting** includes jousting and sword games. Horses and riders wear brightly colored costumes and even armor. **Civil War events** reconstruct activities, skills, and battles from the American Civil War (between 1861 and 1865.) **Cowboy mounted shooting** recreates the excitement of the American frontier. Costumed riders shoot balloon targets. (Ok, so the balloons are not period-accurate!)

The Virtual Arena

Communication via the internet allows horsemen who live far apart to compete against each other. Competitors submit videos of themselves and their horse performing specific patterns or jumping courses. A judge will rank all the videos that have been submitted as they would an in-person class.

Some virtual challenges allow riders to submit their mileage and track their progress against a real race or location. For example, the virtual Tevis Cup sends participants photographs and descriptions from the famous 100-mile race as they complete the miles in their own location.

Clubs for Horse-Crazy Kids

The only thing more fun than learning about horses is learning about them with friends! Luckily, there are many organizations from the local to international level that teach horsemanship to kids. **Pony Club** is an international organization that uses a proven education system to teach all aspects of riding, competing and horse care. **Dressage4Kids**, D4K, centers around dressage. **4-H** teaches many other aspects of farming,

animal care, and healthy living along with horsemanship. The **FFA** (Future Farmers of America) focuses more broadly on agriculture, leadership training, and career preparation.

Do you love games? The United States Mounted Games Association and Mounted Games Across America are two organizations that sponsor clinics and competitions all about games. Both groups are open to riders of all ages. You can keep gaming with your friends as a grown-up!

Many breed associations sponsor youth programs. Often you can participate without owning a horse of that breed. Some associations offer educational materials or special awards. Some even grant college scholarships!

Local riding clubs can be great sources for fun, friendship, and learning. Ask your instructor if she knows of one that might be perfect for you. They often rely on word-of-mouth advertising, so ask about them at a feed store or veterinary office.

More Than Just Riding

Showing is so more than just time in the saddle! Take out your horse journal to explore some thoughts and possibilities. What skills do you need to practice for the show? Break it down to the smallest steps. What can you do in the barn to improve your bond with your horse? How can you strengthen your memory for patterns and courses? Maybe you need to write them down and review them at the trailer before you ride.

What exercises can you do on your own to improve your fitness? When we talk about fitness, we need to address both our

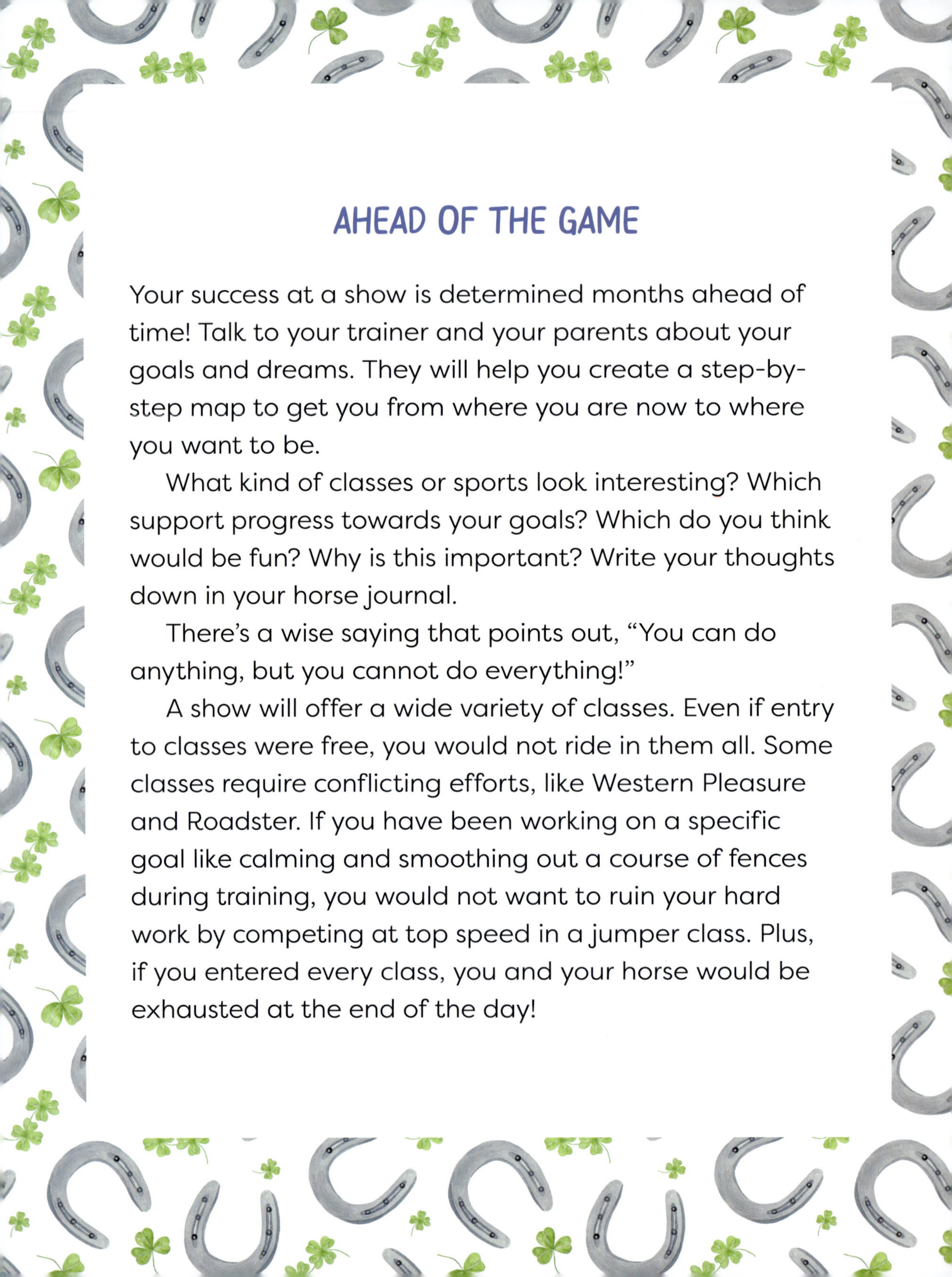

AHEAD OF THE GAME

Your success at a show is determined months ahead of time! Talk to your trainer and your parents about your goals and dreams. They will help you create a step-by-step map to get you from where you are now to where you want to be.

What kind of classes or sports look interesting? Which support progress towards your goals? Which do you think would be fun? Why is this important? Write your thoughts down in your horse journal.

There's a wise saying that points out, "You can do anything, but you cannot do everything!"

A show will offer a wide variety of classes. Even if entry to classes were free, you would not ride in them all. Some classes require conflicting efforts, like Western Pleasure and Roadster. If you have been working on a specific goal like calming and smoothing out a course of fences during training, you would not want to ruin your hard work by competing at top speed in a jumper class. Plus, if you entered every class, you and your horse would be exhausted at the end of the day!

On the other hand, sometimes entering different divisions can support your goals. It can be great fun to learn new skills! Remember that a horse show brings the added challenge of stress and excitement, so if you want to try a new division, practice first. Your instructor is your best ally in making these decisions.

Different classes demand different styles of tack, clothing, and presentation. Learn what your sport requires. Practice necessary skills such as mane braiding or banding long before show time. Keep your tack clean and in good condition, so show preparation is a cinch.

Your horse will need to be as healthy as he can. Make sure he's up to date on routine health. Will he be due for any appointments right before the show? Any changes in routine can affect your horse's attitude or performance. If he is supposed to get a trim or be dewormed immediately before a show, reschedule the appointment a little bit earlier. Is your farrier due just after the show? Schedule the appointment for the week before so your horse doesn't throw a shoe at the last minute.

The right preparation makes show day easy fun. Start planning your perfect experience today!

body and our mind, especially our emotions! You will be under a lot of pressure at the show. Skills that seem to be second nature at home may seem to disappear. Your horse will be distracted as well.

Put together a game plan ahead of time. Write down all the challenges you imagine might arise at the show, and the emotions those challenges might make you feel. Then think of as many ways as you can to overcome them. Reread the parts in this book about using visualization while controlling your breathing and directing your energy, even when you are nervous. Your horse will thank you! Ask your instructor for additional ideas.

Starting now, put these ideas into practice. Your emotions are like muscles: the more you practice the feelings you want, the stronger they will be, even under the pressure of a horse show!

10

Live the Horse Life!

You are still a horse-crazy kid, but you are no longer an absolute beginner! Now you know horses inside and out. You know what makes a good horseman, and you are well on your way to becoming one.

In 2023 in the United States alone:

- There were 7.25 million horses.
- The equine industry generated $122 billion.
- 1.74 million people worked in the equine industry.
- 1.6 million households owned at least one horse.

Horses are serious business!

But maybe that's not enough. Maybe you want to spend your entire life with horses. Maybe you want to pursue a career that centers around horses.

This chapter will speak directly to you! You will learn how to harness your strengths and your weaknesses. You may even learn of some interesting careers that you didn't realize include horses.

Throughout this chapter, you will meet a bunch of horse-crazy kids that kept horses in their lives when they grew up. You may see yourself in parts of their stories. They will share things you can do right now to help launch the horse career of your dreams. Learn from their successes and challenges how to live the horse life as an adult.

Around the Farm

Many careers include everyday involvement with horses. A barn manager coordinates feeding, health care, and scheduling for all the horses in the stable. She maintains the buildings, pastures, and fencing. She manages any employees. She communicates with owners to answer any questions.

BRAINSTORMING YOUR BEST HORSE CAREER

Instead of reading about a career and deciding if it appeals to you, start with thinking about you. What do you love to be around? What do you love to do? How do you love to feel? What skills do people say you are good at? Write these in your horse journal, with plenty of space around the words. On the next page, write down the things you dislike being around and doing, the feelings you want to avoid, and the chores you dread.

As you read about different careers, write them down next to the skills or feelings they support. Do not worry about doing it perfectly, or crossing out things that might be wrong. Just keep the ideas flowing. This is called brainstorming.

Write down any new or unexpected thoughts that come up during this process.

Grooms are responsible for all aspects of horse care, from brushing and tacking to traveling to shows or races. Professional braiders specialize in braiding horses' manes and tails for horse shows. Breeders study bloodlines and performance to plan the best matches for mares and stallions. Rescue operators save horses from horrible situations, nurse them back to good health, and find them safe, loving homes.

If you love meeting new people, consider a career with the public. Riding instructors and coaches teach beginners how to ride, and help advanced students get even better. Pony Party operators take ponies to children's birthday parties or other events for short rides. Carriage drivers take people on peaceful rides or to special events in beautiful horse-drawn carriages.

Inga Fricke, Attorney and Horse Rescuer

I doubted my ability to actually pursue my passion as a career—I wasn't good at math or science, so being a biologist or a vet or another animal 'champion' seemed out of the question. I was good at writing (and arguing!), so I settled for becoming an environmental attorney.

As soon as I got my first official job, I started not only taking riding lessons but volunteering at local animal shelters and wildlife rehabilitation centers to get my animal 'fix.' I had no idea there were so many animals that were ill, injured, and homeless who needed help, and it felt good to do what I could for them. After a few years, I realized that I loved my volunteer work much more than I loved my career, so I took a leap and decided to work in an animal shelter full time. Since then, hundreds of horses have come and gone through those doors, and I could not be more proud.

As executive director of an animal-control facility, I deal with situations that involve charging people with animal cruelty or neglect, so having a legal

REAL HORSE, REAL RIDERS

Christie used to show up at a local university's polo games. She volunteered to hot-walk horses in between chukkers (periods). One player saw how devoted Christie was and introduced her to his mother Shirley, the DC (leader) of the local Pony Club. Shirley loaned Christie a pony and helped her get started in Pony Club. Eventually Christie became a trainer and riding instructor and remains one to this day! That opportunity would not have been possible unless Christie showed up every week in all kinds of weather to work hard with the horses she loved.

background is very helpful. And of course, having legal skills has helped me work with legislators to create and improve laws to benefit animals around the country.

You do not need a degree to put your passions to use for animals. Animal organizations are just like any other business: they need accountants, human resources experts, marketers, event planners, and business managers to keep them running. Nowadays so much of our work is accomplished through social media, so if you like the idea of crafting posts about animals waiting for adoption, posting pictures of adoptable pets, and sharing information with pet owners in the community, you can be a social media coordinator. If you prefer working out with the public, you can run a shelter's community outreach program. And if you're great at writing or storytelling, you can use those skills to help generate the donations that pay for the animals' care. There's almost no talent that cannot be put to good use for the animals!

In the Saddle

If you become a skilled rider, you may enjoy a career that keeps you in the saddle for hours every day. Trainers in all sports and disciplines teach horses to be good partners and athletes. Professional riders and drivers train and show clients' horses. Horse show judges use the skills they have learned over a lifetime of riding to evaluate competitors at horse shows.

Ranch hands work cattle from horseback. Guides lead trail rides or hunting trips for several hours or several weeks. Mounted police officers keep the peace from horseback. Search and rescue riders find people lost in remote areas. Park rangers patrol hundreds of acres of forest and range.

Racetracks have many riding career opportunities. Exercise riders train and condition horses to run their fastest. Jockeys ride horses in races. Outriders lead racehorses to the starting gate, and catch loose horses when jockeys fall.

Susan Horn, Horse Show Judge

I'm qualified to judge after over fifty-five years of showing Hunter-Jumpers, owning an equestrian facility and managing horse shows at the farm. Judging seemed the next logical step in my career after the farm was sold. I could still work in the horse industry without the day-to-day commitment of owning a farm.

The normal show day is about ten to twelve hours long for a judge, so a big task is staying focused and organized with the judge's score cards though out the day. Sometimes a judge may hold four to six cards open so the divisions can progress efficiently. Since horse shows are generally held outdoors, if the weather is extremely hot, cold, or rainy it can be a challenge. I always remind myself that a day doing what I love is better than a day at a traditional office, hands down.

The advice I would give a young person is to sit at the ring and watch all the rounds, all day, and see if they can follow the scoring. Sit at the ring at every horse show. Keep watching and asking questions. Try to see why the winners are winning! Watch the top professionals, expose yourself to as many clinics and instructors as possible, and ride with the best professionals you can afford because this is where connections are made. Attend the top horse shows or watch on a live stream. Try to follow the scoring.

Hands-on Horse Health

Equine health care offers many exciting career opportunities. Veterinarians keep horses healthy and handle emergencies. Surgeons specialize in performing operations to save horses' lives. Veterinary technicians help veterinarians run tests, perform procedures, and manage the office.

Some veterinarians offer acupuncture, a treatment using special needles. Others offer chiropractic care, adjusting horses' bones and joints. Equine dentists "float" (file) horses' teeth. Some states allow specialization in acupuncture, chiropractic, and dentistry without having to go to veterinary school.

Massage therapists keep horses' muscles loose and relaxed, ready to perform at their best. Farriers trim hooves, set horseshoes, and create specialized shoes to treat injuries or deformities.

Dr. Jordan Kiviniemi-Moore, DVM

I am an equine ambulatory veterinarian, which means I am a doctor for horses on the farms where they live. The most unusual aspect of my job is that we can provide pretty sophisticated medical care working in a barn or field with equipment that we drive around in a truck! It is very cool to take digital X-rays in a barn and instantly see the images, and to do minor surgeries in a field, especially when you realize that in humans, this would all be done in a clinic or hospital.

I always wanted to be a veterinarian because I love animals, science, and medicine. I was homeschooled, so I had extra opportunities to pursue subjects that were especially interesting for me! I was able to take extra science classes which were helpful to prepare me for the college level classes required for entry to veterinary school. Since I wasn't restricted to a normal classroom schedule, I had the opportunity to start volunteering several days a week at a small animal clinic.

When I was in college I knew I needed to get more experience with large animals and I did an internship at an equine rehabilitation facility. This made me realize that I loved equine medicine!

The best way to explore being an equine veterinarian is to shadow or volunteer with an equine veterinarian! This may be challenging when you are very young, as working with horses is dangerous and some veterinarians and clinics cannot allow people under eighteen to work with them.

In the meantime, try shadowing or volunteering with a small animal

SETBACKS AND STEPPING STONES

Sometimes a setback is actually a stepping stone to move you further towards your goals than you can imagine. "A major roadblock for me was when I wasn't accepted to the internship program I really wanted after I graduated vet school," said Dr. Jordan. "Instead, I ended up doing a rotating internship (year of more specialized training for newly graduated doctors) at a teaching hospital where I rotated between the field care, medicine, and surgery services. This experience absolutely made me a better veterinarian, and I eventually became a veterinarian for the practice where I'd always wanted to work."

veterinarian, or working in a barn or stable. You do not have to be an expert rider to be a horse vet, but it helps to be comfortable around horses and as you spend more time with them you will learn more about normal horse behavior and common injuries and ailments. Do not be afraid to ask questions!

Take a lot of science classes when you are in school. Veterinary school is like medical school but for multiple species of animals, so it is great to start learning biology and chemistry early on!"

Off the Farm

Not all horse careers happen in a barn! Many jobs are critical to the industry and give you the chance to help horses. Accountants help horse farms and businesses with finances. Marketers use their smarts and creativity to advertise. Real estate agents who specialize in equestrian properties help buyers find the perfect farm for their needs.

Auctioneers sell horses for top dollar with their sing-song chants. Professional haulers transport horses around the country. Nutrition specialists help feed companies design new feeds and help horse owners choose the best feed for their horse. Farmers grow grain and hay.

Researchers work in the laboratory to make new discoveries with the help of trained laboratory technicians. Paleontologists and archeologists study ancient artifacts or search the world for new discoveries.

Dr. Heather Daniell, Lifetime Horsewoman and Founder and CEO LoGI Food Technologies

"I am a food tech entrepreneur. I'm a scientist by training, having a PhD in organic chemistry. After leaving grad school, I had left academic science, but I guess I couldn't keep my experimental brain from trying to problem solve. Plus, I think it is also pretty fun to develop something brand new and grow that into a business.

I run a food business where we've turned salads into a range of chips. I developed a patented process that enabled us to remove the starch or sugar binders from dried foodstuffs—everything from horse and pet food to people snacks too.

The inspiration was actually a horse of mine who had gastric ulcers. Knowing that he wasn't supposed to eat large amounts of sugar or starch, I set about figuring how to make the same durable foods but without the starch or sugar. My first product was actually a horse treat.

If you are a horse-crazy kid, make sure that you find time to fit in your studies. Having the foundation of a good degree will give you options later on, even if you think initially you want to pursue a horsey career. It will also help to give you the skills to manage your own horsey business from marketing to finance etc. Or it may give you skills so that you can work in the horse industry (for instance horse products business) but not necessarily with horses.

I think the key is to be realistic about what you want to wake up and do every morning.

In the Arts

If you enjoy the arts, there is a horse career for you! Writers create stories, books, and articles about horses. Journalists report on horse shows, races, and happenings in the horse world.

Artists create paintings, illustrations for books and articles, and portraits of horses. They may make horsey crafts.

Photographers take pictures at horse events, or on private farms. They may take senior pictures for a high school student and her beloved horse, or take advertising pictures to promote a trainer, a stallion, or a horse for sale.

Horse-crazy artists can use their skills to change the world. They might bring attention to endangered breeds in remote countries or highlight a challenging situation.

Karen McLain, Artist

I am a professional artist, known mostly for painting wild horses. When I visited my first herd of wild horses in 2009, the experience transformed my art. I saw the beauty, power, and risk inherent in living wild in nature.

While I am painting in the field, I have my camera on my shoulder to take photos or short video for studio painting reference. I also start each painting with a quick gesture sketch. When I return to the studio, I have photos/video, sketches, and a field study painting. These are what I base larger paintings on.

When I was a kid, I was always active in art and loved the outdoors. So, outdoor painting is the best of both worlds. In addition to having a degree in art, I have had the opportunity to take workshops from many artists that I respect. This ongoing instruction allows me to remain challenged, and I always learn something new.

One thing that I would encourage would be the development of curiosity. This maintains our desire to keep learning. Be prepared for opportunities to discover new insight and skill, and enjoy the adventure!

In the Spotlight

If you love entertainment, you can find a horsey career! Movie wranglers organize, train, and handle the horses on set. Stunt riders execute daring feats on horseback. Extras ride horses in the background. Actors at dinner theaters such as Medieval Times dress as knights and perform in the saddle several times a day.

If you enjoy speaking with clarity, consider a voice career. Record audio books about horses. Announce at horse shows. "Call" the action as it happens in horse races.

Ray Ingandela, Show Announcer

At my first rally as a Pony Club Parent, I was in the Ring Crew. We schlepped jump standards and rails. I knew it was not my favorite thing to do—especially in the hot, humid weather.

One day, I noticed the announcer. He looked like he had just flown in from another world. He was not sweating. He was nattily dressed. His clothes and hands were clean. *Hmmm,* I thought, *Now, that's the job I want!*

I discovered I was pretty comfortable with announcing since I had been an Air Force pilot and had to talk on radios as I flew. And I learned a little about announcing at every subsequent rally. The most important thing I discovered was that, even though I was not the organizer, secretary, steward, or judge, I could set the tone for the event with my voice.

Be Yourself!

You have special talents that no one else does. Keep working to strengthen your skills. Focus on what you love to do.

Sometimes a career in horses leads in many different directions. Do not be afraid to explore or change focus when your interests and circumstances evolve. With some ingenuity, even a bad situation can lead to unexpected opportunities!

Anastasia Talbott, "For the Love of Ribbons" Craft Store

My parents told me if I ever wanted a horse, I would need to finance it myself and figure out how to keep it. From a very early age, I learned about how to manage money and keep as much saved as possible. I sold brownies to buy my first horse at the age of twelve.

Having this value instilled in me from a young age made me want to do more and achieve more with horses and in my own personal goals. It made me value horsemanship as much if not more than actual riding and showing.

I have done many jobs in the industry from breaking colts to stall mucker, and mainly now a barn manager. I parallel that job with making art with horse-show ribbons. This came about when Covid lockdowns were in effect. I had seen some wreaths on Pinterest and thought I could replicate them.

I posted my wreath on one of the local Facebook pages. It went from there! I had to brainstorm and come up with new items to make. Some things I made never really sold, others took off with thousands of likes and orders to follow.

What I love most about this is that I can help folks bring their ribbons and hard work out of boxes and attics and display them. I honestly struggle the most with staying on top of spreadsheets and orders. I strongly encourage if you plan on doing anything with social media as your main outreach learning everything you can about that platform. Pay attention in your Excel classes and learn what formulas can really help you with shortcuts."

Top Tips for a Horse-Crazy Career

1. **Write a list** of careers that appeal to you. Which ones are a good fit, given your strengths and interests? For example, if you love math and horse racing, you might love being an accountant for a famous Thoroughbred breeding farm. Update this list as you learn more about different careers with horses. Follow your curiosity!
2. **Keep your eyes open** for unusual or unexpected horsey careers. Ask your friends, your instructor, and horse professionals like your vet and farrier for suggestions. Add all the ideas to your list, even if they do not appeal to you right now.
3. **Become a people person.** If you're shy, it can be hard to reach out to people. Most people want to help. You never know what doors might open! If you are friendly, honest, and polite, most people are happy to help. After all, they were once horse-crazy kids too!
4. **Take school seriously.** While your classes may not seem to have anything to do with a horse career, they will teach you skills that you will need to be successful out of the saddle. Math, English, and science are vital in running your own horse business. Furthermore, your school classes will teach you to think and problem solve in new and helpful ways.
5. **Keep showing up.** Take advantage of every opportunity to work around horses. People notice more than just your

riding ability. People pay attention to things like a strong work ethic and a positive attitude. You never know who will notice and where it will lead.

6. **Be open to unexpected opportunities!** After a childhood filled with horses, shows, and championships, Mary chose a career in video production. When the director of a film she was working on needed a stunt rider for a sidesaddle sequence, Mary volunteered. She had never ridden sidesaddle before, but she didn't let that stop her! She caught on quickly and is now immortalized in film.
7. **Adjust and keep going.** Life circumstances change, but creative horse lovers adapt and move forward. Michael was a full-time trainer and instructor. As a horse-crazy kid, he had gotten in trouble for doodling horses in the margins of his notebook! When health problems kept him away from the barn, he began creating and selling vibrant paintings of horses.
8. **Gain real world experience.** Nothing beats hands-on learning! Many riding schools have working student or intern programs. You will work hard, but you will gain valuable skills working with horses. You will learn the business of horses from the ground up.
9. **Learn about business.** It is not enough to be a good rider. You will need to be a good businessperson. Google your local business laws and ask a trusted adult to help fact check. Tell your instructor and other horse professionals you are interested in learning more about business, and

ask what requirements they have to meet. Learn about insurance and taxes. Find out what is involved with hiring employees. You may find you love learning about business so much that you decide to become an equine business consultant.

10. **Start now!** What are some things you can do right now? Perhaps you can groom a horse to a show-ring shine or polish tack like a pro. If you love to sew, you can repair torn blankets. If you enjoy braiding your friends' hair, you can braid manes and tails for horse shows. If you are still a beginner, practice, practice, practice!
11. **Take baby steps.** If a career you dream of seems out of reach, break it down into smaller steps. Think about information you will need to know and skills you will need to master. What is something you can do right now to move towards those goals? For example, imagine you dream of becoming an equine artist. You do not need to go to art school to get started. Sharpen your pencil and start practicing. Perhaps you can start a little side business sketching horses.

You will face obstacles and challenges. Remember, you are not in this alone! Be courageous in reaching out and asking adults who have followed the path that you want to travel. As long as you are your polite, friendly self, most people will be happy to help you!

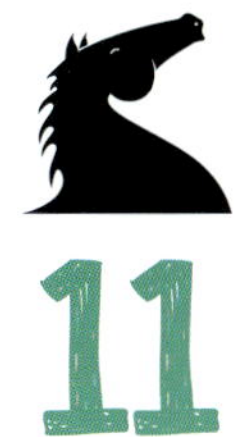

11

What You Want Your Parents to Know

This chapter may be at the end of this book, but it just might be the most important chapter of all! Your parents want what's best for you. They will be your biggest cheerleaders. They will pour out emotional and financial support for you to achieve your dreams. This chapter will help them understand why supporting your horse passion not only makes you happy, but can help you grow into an even better person.

Maybe your parents just need to know enough about horses to help you chart an action plan to turn your dream into reality. Maybe they will be so excited to learn about horses that they want to read this whole book with you! Either way, this chapter is written specifically for them. For the rest of this chapter, when I say "you," I'm talking to your parents!

Hi, Parents!

Congratulations on being the parents of a horse-crazy kid! While it may seem strange or even overwhelming at times, the horsey life brings immense meaning and value to your child's life. Provided children learn safe, correct techniques on the ground and in the saddle, horses will help every aspect of your child's development. The lessons learned in the barn and riding arena, cloaked as "fun," teach enduring life skills.

Emotionally, horses teach kindness, calmness, and patience. Your child learns to be responsible for a creature outside of herself. She learns accountability to you, her instructor, and the barn staff. A positive "kid culture" in a program develops strong, caring social skills.

Mentally, horses can encourage a love of learning that subjects at school might not inspire. Ambitions for advancement in training or the show ring teach goal-setting and logical progression. Competitions instill skills like preparation, sportsmanship, and grace in both winning and losing.

Horse riding is by definition a team sport in the sense that the rider has to look after her partner's training and well-being. While many riding competitions are performed individually, team competitions teach additional interpersonal skills.

Most Pony Club and 4-H activities are team-based, even if the horse and rider are alone in the arena. Sports such as polocrosse and team penning involve all the team members on the field at the same time working together to achieve the goal.

Physically, riding develops core fitness, suppleness, balance, and coordination. More intense sports such as eventing, with strength and cardio aspects, can also inspire interests in other activities as cross-training.

"My Son Wants to Ride"

Fantastic! Many of the top international competitors are men. A riding school with male role models will be ideal. Some boys, especially young boys,

REAL RIDERS, REAL PARENTS

Angela is very blunt when describing why she was willing to pour family resources into lessons and horse shows. When her horse-crazy daughters were only nine and seven years old, Angela had long-term vision. She thought if the girls were already deeply focused on their horsemanship transitioning into their teenage years they would have less time or interest for distractions such as boys, alcohol, and drugs.

With shows to prep for on Friday nights, Angela knew the girls would be at the barn braiding manes and stuffing hay bags rather than out looking for trouble. With new goals to work towards with their beloved horses, traditional teenage temptations would have far less power. Angela found a local riding school with top-notch instruction and a strong youth show team. Her now-teenagers thrive in a fun, positive community.

lose interest with the kind of detail-oriented focus that some girls thrive on. Try to involve your son in an aspect of the sport with a "purpose"—mounted games, fox chasing, and trail type sports such as endurance riding, can capture his attention. A good instructor will direct the right balance between fun and formal instruction, developing correct equitation almost as a side effect rather than the sole focus.

"My Child Has Special Needs"

Riding has proven to have profound developmental impacts—physically, mentally, and emotionally. The Professional Association of Therapeutic Horsemanship International (PATH International) has strict standards for certification for instructors and facilities.

If your child does not have special needs, consider getting him involved with a local program as a volunteer. Become a volunteer yourself! Volunteers enthusiastically say that they get as much out of the program as the riders.

"Why Should I Invest So Much? She Might Not Stick With It!"

While some horse-crazy kids decide to pursue intense competition or a later career in horses, neither are benchmarks for "success" with horses. Instead, look to the valuable skills and life lessons that shape a character into adulthood. In the good times, horses are an inspiration for learning and growth. During the inevitable dark times, horses can literally save lives.

Finding a Facility

The best thing you can do for your horse-crazy child is to find a reputable riding school. Books can teach a lot about riding and horse care, but nothing beats the guidance, supervision, and wisdom of an experienced instructor. She will provide a safe, supportive atmosphere, a roadmap to achieve goals within your family's parameters, and communication tailored to your child's strongest learning style. Sit down with your child and compile a list of "musts," "must nots," and "would-be-nice-ifs." Your child's instructor will be a major influence on her, so invest the time to find a great fit.

Google local stables. Check the yellow pages, if your area still has one—some amazing instructors still lean on old-school advertising. Ask the staff at your local feed and tack stores. Check their community bulletin boards.

Many of the best teachers and riding schools are so popular they do not need to advertise. Visit a few local horse shows

REAL HORSES, REAL RIDERS

Trina was raised in an equestrian family. While she rode horses from an early age, it was clear that horses were not "her thing." As an adult, Trina shared the impact of her horse time in an emotional letter to her former riding instructor. These are her words.

"I was introduced to horses at a time where I was extremely afraid of authority in every sense. You helped me understand the power balance of nature and humans, which I consider to be one of the greatest gifts I've ever gotten in my life. I remember being TERRIFIED . . . and yet you still somehow made it fun. You were a staple every single week even more so than a couple of semi-distant family members. You changed my life for the better. You are one of the most amazing teachers I've ever come across in my life."

In high school, Trina suffered bullying and abuse. She kept her struggles a secret, even from her parents. Her mental health suffered badly. She shared how her instructor's emotional support carried her through these dark times.

"Talking to you has shed a light on how people are supposed to be treated," wrote Trina. "You mean the world to me."

Trina's parents' investment in riding lessons produced far greater returns than success in the saddle. It produced success in life.

(your horse-crazy kid will be thrilled!) and look for the groups of riders who seem confident, competent, and happy. Find out who is teaching them.

Locate the closest branch of Pony Club or 4-H in your area. These are nationwide organizations with an outstanding track record for safety, fun, and education. Being a part of such a like-minded community can change the trajectory of your child's horsemanship arc. The community will be able to recommend local instructors and may open the door to unexpected opportunities.

While convenience is a factor, location should not be the only consideration. A stable offering an extensive program that will carry your child towards her goals is worth driving a little farther.

England and many European nations require instructors to pass a certification exam. In the United States, certification is optional. While many fine instructors choose not to certify, certification can be a sign that the instructor takes her business seriously enough to invest additional time, money, and education. If the instructors you are considering are certified, google the parent organization to get a feel for what is covered and if she is a good fit for your child.

The Stable Tour

A facility does not need to be fancy. It does need to be safe, friendly, and educational. Most businesses prefer that you call in advance to set up a tour. Horse farms, especially those with thriving lesson programs, are extremely busy with tightly-run routines.

Write down any questions you have so you remember to ask during your tour. If the staff member cannot answer a question, he should let you know he will get back to you.

Are all of the structures in good repair? While peeling paint is not necessarily a sign of a second-rate program, jutting nails and broken fence boards are a big red flag!

Do all of the horses look healthy and happy? Do stalls show signs of regular cleaning? Are the work areas organized and

tidy? Is the arena footing safe? Overly dusty, slick, rocky, or concrete-hard surfaces can cause accidents and injury.

Watch a lesson, or several, being taught if you can. Do horses and riders look like they are safe and having fun? Fun may look different in an intensely competitive program, but expressions should look appropriate!

Some states have tax or other business laws that apply to riding schools. Many states have laws that limit liability of riding schools in the case of an accident, but that does not eliminate the need for an instructor or facility to carry liability insurance. Investigate your state laws, and if the riding school complies. Businesses that cut corners in one area are apt to cut them in many.

The right barn for your child must be the right barn for your family. Your final decision will probably be a blend of location, education, and economics.

Head First: The Importance of Helmets

Your child will probably tell you that she needs all of the clothing and equipment in the tack catalog! Luckily, she needs only a few key items to get started safely and comfortably.

Your first—and most important—purchase will be a helmet that meets or exceeds the current American Standards for Testing and Materials/Safety Equipment Institute (ASTM/SEI) standards. This helmet must be designed specifically for riding: the impact to the skull and brain from a fall from a horse are very different from a fall off a bicycle, for example.

Helmets are readily available in a vast array of styles from farm supply stores, tack shops, and online. Prices vary widely, from under $50 to several hundred dollars. The best helmet will fail if not adjusted correctly to fit your child's head. Good salespeople, your riding instructor, or another trusted horseperson can help ensure correct fit. Instructions enclosed with a new helmet will also give you step-by-step directions.

Most manufacturers recommend replacing a helmet after five years. This may sound like a sales racket, but it has been proven that the materials break down over time, especially in direct sunlight. Helmets should be replaced after a fall, or even a bad drop. The materials inside the helmet are designed to compress to slow the brain's impact against the skull. Once compressed, protective ability is lost. Helmets should also be replaced after any exposure to chemicals and solvents.

Never purchase a helmet used. You have no way of knowing the helmet's history. Your child's life is too valuable to compromise in the name of saving a few dollars.

Many tack stores discount riding helmets for International Helmet Awareness Day. IHAD was founded in 2010 in honor of Courtney King-Dye, an Olympic equestrian who suffered a traumatic brain injury when her horse tripped and fell. Courtney was riding at a walk on a well-trained horse, highlighting that life-threatening accidents happen regardless of skill level of horse and rider. Do not wait until IHAD to purchase a helmet for your aspiring young Olympian, but keep it in mind if you are casually looking for a routine replacement or an upgrade on a budget.

Some riding programs are rooted in traditions that do not mandate helmets. If your barn does not require helmets, insist that your child wear one anyway. No good barn will object. Indeed, most insurance companies will not cover an accident if a helmet was not worn. As we said before, if your instructor does not carry liability insurance, find another one.

Completing the Outfit

Different barns may have different dress codes, whether spoken or implied. Always ask your instructor for requirements or suggestions. He can also give you tips for the best tack shops in the area.

Safety vests are becoming more prevalent, particularly in jumping and speed sports. Some stables require them for all students. Pony Club requires them for cross-country riding. Modern safety vests are comfortable and can prevent or minimize injury in the case of the inevitable fall.

Your child will need sturdy footwear that goes above the ankle for protection against an accidental stomp or knock. The boot should have a slight heel (to prevent the foot from sliding through the stirrup and getting caught) and a non-aggressive tread (to allow it to fall freely from the stirrup in case of a tumble).

Expensive tall boots are unnecessary and are often quickly outgrown. Paddock boots (English) or ropers or lacers (western) are acceptable and far more affordable. Hybrid boots that are as comfortable as your favorite pair of sneakers but also meet the criteria for safety in the saddle are a terrific alternative, especially if your child will also be spending long days on her feet in the barn.

Long pants are a must. Blue jeans are acceptable. If your child is riding English, she may find the seams painful. Riding tights are a comfortable alternative, as are the more traditional jodhpurs or breeches. Tights that are not made specifically for riding may be too slippery, or have seams in uncomfortable places. If your child rides English and he has an ankle-height boot, he will also want a pair of half chaps to protect the inside of his calves from the rubbing of the stirrup leathers. (The fenders of a western saddle generally do not cause rubbing.)

Riding gloves can be a welcome addition as your child advances, particularly in the summer when sweat can cause the reins to slip, or in winter when every layer counts.

Good gear can be pricey and kids grow quickly. Luckily, most online and brick-and-mortar tack stores have seasonal clearance sales. For everything but helmets, parents can also take advantage of a strong secondhand market. Many riding schools host an "outgrown exchange." Some areas are fortunate enough to have consignment tack stores. Many of these tack stores offer an online option. Even if they do not have their inventory online, some are willing to help you out. It is worth a phone call!

The internet can be like the wild west. Be especially diligent when purchasing from social media marketplaces or auction sites.

A Horse of Her Own . . .

Every horse-crazy kid wishes for nothing more than a horse of her own. Horses require knowledgeable care, significant land, and a robust budget. Even if you have the land and knowledge, is this the best step? Particularly in the beginning, your time and money are best spent on quality instruction with level-appropriate horses.

"A rising tide raises all ships" goes the proverb. A strong equestrian community will bring education, support, and comradery. Kids let loose to learn on their own are far more inclined to be intimidated, injured, or lose interest.

Some old-timers brag about learning by the seat of their pants or recount getting dumped off the "devil pony" until they learned how to stick. But for every old-timer's success story, there are scores of adults who missed out on the joy and fulfillment of horsemanship because terrifying experiences convinced them to quit. Successful, lifelong equestrians are far more likely to have started off on a quiet, well-trained "schoolmaster" with a knowledgeable instructor balancing confidence building with just enough challenge to keep riding exciting.

The perfect beginner horse has plenty of "mileage," that is, positive training and show or performance experience. He "can take a joke," that is, he tolerates his rider's mistakes during the learning process. He may have some age- or work-related issues which will require nutritional supplements or veterinary maintenance. Despite his limitations, he is invaluable in helping your child develop solid skills and soaring confidence.

Your child will outgrow that perfect first horse both in height and in ability fairly quickly. It is not fair to push the horse beyond his athletic abilities. He is perfect for the next up-and-coming beginner, while your child can move up to a more appropriate mount.

As your child progresses, there are several viable options to ownership. Consider allowing him to take additional weekly lessons. Ask your instructor if half-leasing or full-leasing a school horse is a possibility. Private owners also offer their horses in leases, with various financial arrangements. Many Pony Clubs have beloved mounts that stay within the club. As riders progress beyond the horse's abilities, the horse moves on to younger, less experienced riders.

Once your young equestrian has shown commitment and developed competence, you may decide to take the leap into horse ownership. That is a topic for its own book! Research as much as you can. Include experts such as your child's instructor or club leader in the process. Invest in a pre-purchase examination regardless of the horse's price. Make sure any agreements, including all costs, responsibilities, and warrantees, are captured in writing.

Horse ownership is a huge commitment, both financially and emotionally. In the right circumstances, it is supremely rewarding. However, ownership is not essential for your horse-crazy kid to have fulfilling equestrian life.

Horses capture kids' hearts and transform their lives. Supporting your horse-crazy child means muddy boots, early mornings, and a whole new vocabulary—but it also means nurturing responsibility, confidence, and a deep connection to the natural world. Whether your child dreams of lessons, leasing, or just reading every horse book on the shelf, you are her biggest cheerleader. Done right, horse-crazy kids grow into responsible, empathic adults. That's a win for any parent!

About the Author

Kirsten Lee was born a horse-crazy kid! She is a lifelong riding instructor, judge, and horse trainer. She is certified through the American Riding Instructors Association in Dressage and Eventing and is a United States Pony Club Graduate "A." Kirsten and her students have competed successfully up to the national level in Dressage, Combined Training, Hunter/Jumper, and Polocrosse. When she's not in the saddle, Kirsten can be found on her farm in wild, wonderful West Virginia, or at www.wvhorsetrainer.com and www.bestbeginnersguidetohorses.com.

Index